Amitabh Bachchan
Reflections on a Star Image

Amitabh Bachchan

Reflections on a Star Image

Susmita Dasgupta

B L O O M S B U R Y

NEW DELHI • LONDON • OXFORD • NEW YORK • SYDNEY

First published in India 2018

ISBN 978 93 86826 15 2
2 4 6 8 10 9 7 5 3 1

Bloomsbury Publishing India Pvt. Ltd
Second Floor, LSC Building No.4
DDA Complex, Pocket C – 6 & 7, Vasant Kunj
New Delhi 110070
www.bloomsbury.com

Typeset by Manipal Digital Systems
Printed and bound in India by Replika Press Pvt. Ltd.

Dedication

To my parents, Siba Prasad and Amita for letting me have the freedom to be me

and

my childhood friend, Madhuri, because most of what follows are my conversations with her when we both were going to school and Amitabh was just rising.

Dedication

Acknowledgment

Sanjit Vaghel, a young friend is the main force behind this book because it was he who introduced Praveen Tiwari of Bloomsbury and me for a possible book on steel. By the time Praveen met me I had already committed my manuscript on steel to another publisher. Since I did not want Sanjit to be disappointed, I promised Praveen another of my secretly developing manuscript consisting a set of existential pieces on Amitabh Bachchan. These pieces are very far from what a general interest reader would expect from writings on a film star since they speak the language in which fans discuss their favourite stars, a language which is very different from those of gossip magazines or of film studies; the language is that of existential philosophy. I am very grateful that Praveen and Rajiv Beri saw the potential of a book on a popular star written as reflective thought pieces. I must thank Nitin Valecha who looked through the manuscript patiently especially in places where sentences would become so self-absorbed so as to not make any sense to anyone else but the writer.

All the arguments and analyses in the book were developed decades ago in many ruminations and arguments around Amitabh Bachchan in the attic of my friend, Madhuri, alias Dr Sharmishtha Mitra, presently a faculty of English literature and a Milton scholar, when both of us were school students.

I am thankful to Dayada, Madhuri's house help who stood in perspiring queues for advance tickets for Amitabh's releases. Later on, in my journey as an Amitabh scholar, I must thank my friend and companion of three decades, Dr Madhusree Banerjee, to have solidly stood beside me in taking off many of my worries and giving me company in my studies. A scholar depends horribly on her domestic helps and here my gratitude goes to Suraj, Sahadeb and Malati in offering me their fullest cooperation.

My friends, Profs Rakesh Batabyal and Mahalakshmi have been enthusiastic supporters of my project on popular cinema. I must thank Prof Ravindranathan and Dr Resmi Bhaskaran for their belief in my thoughts. Another of my young friend, who is more of family, Dibyendu Chowdhury for being a constant cheer giver in my reflections on Amitabh Bachchan. Avijit Ghosh, the well-known author of Cinema Bhojpuri and 40 Retakes has provided me with serious inputs on popular cinema.

I must mention my brother, Dhiman, who though an automation engineer by profession is a philosopher by vocation. I write this book only because he did not do so; were he to write, his would have been a far better work than mine.

Introduction

The purpose of writing a book analysing the image of Amitabh Bachchan is twofold. One is to introduce the general interest reader to a much higher level of film analysis than either the street corner gossip or the published books on the Hindi popular cinema, which rarely, if ever, have any kind of firm theoretical and empirical support. The other purpose for writing this book is to capture the public attention as the superstar celebrates his 75th birthday and use the hype to introduce a new level of intellectual discourse, not usually associated with entertainment cinema.

The idea of the essays is both to explore who Amitabh Bachchan really is, as well as what he stands for? Amitabh, as a person and Amitabh as a phenomenon are addressed together in the book. It makes little sense to write about a film star unless and until we also have a fine framework of stardom in our mind; we must know why some societies produce stars and some particular type of stars, how does an actor become a star and how the aesthetics of cinema is located within the much wider world that we inhabit beyond the theatre. We may speak pathetically if we are not sensitive to the spirit of the stars, the stars who literally raise us beyond our mundane existence into a higher realm of being, where we can become heroes to ourselves and where we can overcome our constraints of everyday living. We may also fail to see the liberation the stars bring to our minds if we only accuse popular culture of making passive automatons out of us and not acknowledge its emancipatory possibilities.

The essays work around theories of star, theories of cinema, theories of Hindi popular cinema, popular culture and within these coordinates, try to locate the stardom of Amitabh Bachchan in its phenomenal stature. Throughout the essays we keep in mind that Amitabh Bachchan is a game changer as far as the image of a star is concerned. It has been our endeavour to analyse why he has been the towering presence in the Hindi film industry and in what ways was the image of Amitabh Bachchan so different from the general pantheon of the stars.

Contents

Formula of the Star

There is a structure to the Indian popular cinema

The structure of the Indian popular cinema, is fairly similar across the many languages in which it is made. There is a protagonist who desires to lead a simple, run of the mill, and 'normal', mainstream life, but faces numerous problems on her way of attaining this. She may be poor, or lose her parents; she may herself be disabled or may even lose her lover should he die; she may have to raise her children all by herself, or she may be kidnapped, molested or raped. In case of a male star, he may face similar kinds of violence and may have the anxiety of not being able to look after his family, especially his suffering mother or his ailing wife. In the end, the obstacles are all overcome, mostly by putting a face to the obstacles, namely that of a villain, aided by his female counterpart, the vamp. It is quite usual for the Indian popular cinema to engage in a fight with the villain, or chase each other in comic misunderstanding, and finally have all lose ends tie up, problems resolved and the family comes together.

The Idea of Emotional Exhaustion

All this rigmarole of the Indian popular cinema is to entertain holistically, which means that you should be able to sense all the nine rasas as outlined by the ancient Indian text on dramaturgy, *Natyashastra*, in equal proportions. Indeed you should feel the pain of loss, agony of lost love, excitement of a budding romance, pure affection towards children and animals, emotions of family ties, anger towards a villain, abhorrence towards rapists, and fear of a possible accident and the satisfaction of conquering opposition and eventually the nirvana of having attained your end, which is nothing but a peaceful and ordinary life. The Indian popular cinema is emotionally exhausting; exhausting as in being exhaustive and this exhaustion is its entertainment; the participation by its viewers.

Cinematic Formula is like the Rules of a Game

Intelligent people, connoisseurs of art and cinema geniuses have condemned the formula of the Indian popular cinema as trashy and kitsch. Progressive sociologists have found in the formula cinema the rehash of tradition in the form of upholding the conservative idea of the Indian family. But it is important to place the formulaic film in a wider context of India, of a billion people who watch and relish the cinema. Film insiders insist that the formula of the cinema create a kind of anticipation and an idea of what should be, which reinforce a familiar structure of the narratives in the heads of the viewers. Once the structure is all set, the actors' play becomes enjoyable, and the viewer can participate in the play. It is same as watching a game of cricket or football; you can only enjoy when you know the rules of the game very well. It is difficult for a spectator who has no idea of cricket to enjoy the game, for she will not be able to place the actions of the actors in perspective. The formula of the film is akin to the rules of a game. Surely it is difficult to appreciate Sachin Tendulkar without a familiarity with cricket and a good command over the game of tennis helps us appreciate the greatness of Bjorn Borg or of Steffi Graf.

Formula is About the Notion of the Perfect State of Being

But what does the formula say? The formula revolves around the great idea that a person should live a happy and a peaceful life with her spouse, parents, siblings and children and sometimes pet animals. The film begins when conditions are not right to begin with or go awry cracking up this pretty picture and galvanizing protagonists into activity that would help restore the equilibrium.

Star is Central to the Popular Cinema

The popular cinema perhaps across the world is known by the stars who act in them. The star is a protagonist of the story but his/her role does not end within the story. S/he rises again in a similar persona in yet another film, as if in a series of rebirths. The star shows a consistency of character through the roles she plays; making us believe as if it is the same person in different situations of life, giving us various facets of her where she faces a variety of social milieus. Each film presents an opportunity for the star to play out the role and each role assigns some personality traits to the star. The star assumes different avatars in each film she acts in. These traits are integrated into the image of the star; the larger number of attributes a star can integrate into her persona in a consistent way, the greater the image of the star becomes. Stardom is an ability to appear the very same person across different roles, while not compromising on the demands of the roles.

The Movement Image

Deleuze[1] writes in his two volume tracts on cinema that the cinema produces movement of things and humans; the lasting images in cinema are formed out of the movement image; movement being the act of covering space over time, or what is the same thing, the narrative. The movement produces a consciousness which stands all by itself.

Deleuze favours Henri Bergson's understanding of consciousness over Edmund Husserl. According to Husserl, consciousness is consciousness of something, but for Bergson, consciousness is something in itself. The cinema produces the

---

1 Gilles Deleuze. Cinema 1. Continuum. The Athlone Press. London. Paperback Edition. 1992. pp 58-61.

movement image and creates a certain kind of consciousness which is aligned to the movement image. Perhaps in the same way, Wagner's music created its own consciousness of German nationalism; Wagner said nothing about the nation, never articulated the idea of a nation but his music created a consciousness which became receptive to the idea of German nationalism. In this way, the cinema may generate consciousness which is not about something but a consciousness which becomes receptive to the constitution of modern life. If we place the cinema in an industrial society, or in a society of industrial art, then the cinema works in the same milieu in which individualism rules; there is both a heightened sense of individual agency as well as alienation. The cinema engenders a consciousness which is individualistic, containing both the emancipatory sense of agency as well as being alienated.

Star versus Actor

There is a difference between a star and an actor, a star is an actor but being an actor does not make a person into a star. The actor is constituted by her milieu, overpowered by the same, changed by it and is determined by the movement of the milieu. The movement of the star prevails over the movements of other elements in the film. While the movement of the milieu overpowers the movement of the actor so that she is determined by her situation; the star, on the other hand, conquers and overcomes her situation, creatively changing the world with her consciousness. In an actor dominated cinema, where the movement of the milieu is more defining and it outpaces the movement of the star and the director is remembered as the auteur of the film. In a star-based film, it is the star that has the maximum movement and is remembered as the auteur.

The director-led films such as those by Satyajit Ray, Mrinal Sen and even Shyam Benegal are powerful in imageries, cinematic codes and conventions, and the technology of the medium has been explored to the hilt. But the protagonists in these films do not seem to rise above their socially-determined personalities, adapt and even resign to the forces at work upon them. Such films produce great directorial works of art using the industrial technology of the movie, but they do not privilege the star as the persona who rises above the film material and constitutes an indelible impression in the minds of her fans much beyond the frames. The autonomous existence of the star is the crux of the star appeal and it is also the source of popularity of cinema as a medium; directors are compelled to create scripts which extend the persona of the star in a consistent manner. In common parlance, there appears to be two levels of cinema, the art cinema and the commercial cinema. The former is cinema in which directorial efforts dominate, the latter being the cinema of the star, known as commercial cinema for the prospects of being sold like a commercial product.

Star, Popular Culture and Industrial Technology: New Universals

The star is definitely an important part of popular culture, a term which is problematic if it is detached from the modern age of technology. The popular culture, defines John Fiske[2], is one which reaches out to the individual to lure her out of her embeddedness in the social categories, and attaches her into a larger community of persons similar to hers. We observe here the first paradox of popular culture which is a desire to detach from traditional categories and attach to newer universals. In societies such as India's in which the core of historical transformation is determined by a tussle between tradition and modernity, the popular culture helps transformation of the individual from her alignment in a traditional society into a modern one. Film stars are helpful in creating a consciousness which hugely facilitate this transition into modernity.

Professor D.P.Mukherjee[3], known widely as D.P., is the father of Indian sociology, and he places the unit of sociology, neither in

2 John Fiske. Understanding Popular Culture. Routledge Reprint. London. 2009. Pp 14-15

3 D.P.Mukherjee. Personality and Social Sciences. Rupa. Delhi. 2004. pp 30-56.

the family nor in the social structure but in the individual, who as a member of the human collectivities, acts out in everyday life to produce the social structures which characterise societies. The human action emanates from human cognition, a range of decisions, negotiations and strategies with her surroundings. These surroundings could be the nature, economy, interpersonal relations and the wider social powers. While interacting in such varied ways, in varied kinds of social roles, the crux of the individual is not to get fragmented but to hold herself as a consistent being. The consistency of the individual that helps integrate the varieties of individual operations is known as the personality. According to D.P, society is made up of personalities and social change is nothing but attempts at transformation and changes in personalities. If this be so, then the star is a sociological process at its core, attempts at being as well as becoming.

Sayed Mirza's film in 1977, *Arvind Desai ki Ajeeb Dastan*, reveals clearly the fragmentation of the individual when faced with capitalism, market economy, urbanisation, migration, cosmopolitanism, the rise of the nuclear family, and even the emergence of public spaces like the bar, the paying guest accommodation and so on. Arvind Desai's personhood fragments as he encounters his world and the film belongs to its director and the protagonist is a defeated man. On the other hand, a similar film *Shree 420* built exactly upon the same ingredients as above, produces huge stars, Raj Kapoor and Nargis, because they pull off a moral victory over all the above restrictive social forces. The two films, one art and the other commercial, made almost on similar thoughts, produce different results. Raj Kapoor and Nargis emerge as D.P's idea of the personality as the unit of society.

The Movement Image is Best Experienced in the Star

Given the above, we now return to Deleuze's idea of the movement image. The star is a movement image in which neither the milieu nor the personality is of much concern but the image that is constituted out of the star's moving through her milieu. The star is a set of activities and the image in the minds of her fans emerge out of the act of moving. The star's image is then one not of acts but of activity; the more intense the activity, the greater is the image. Does a star who intensifies her bodily movement only become a star? Yes, bodily energy is a major contributing factor towards the creation of a star but movement is enough. Shammi Kapoor in the 1960's or Ranveer Singh post 2016 are stars with intense body movements, but these have not made them into superstars like Rajesh Khanna, Amitabh Bachchan or even Shah Rukh or Salman Khan. Movement must then mean something more.

The movement of the star against resistance provides the real intensity of movement, for as compared to the former, it is the latter, namely the movement against resistance, which gives the possibility of bringing about a change in the situation, or in terms of physics, of displacement. Movement against resistance is drama. Deleuze insists that cinema is about movement and the movement is best attained when it is towards an emergent newness. What makes the cinema new? In terms of the above schema, the new can only come from a new set of resistances and movements, which perhaps can emanate from new kinds of conflicts in the story. New cinema is all about new drama. Popular cinema, brings to light hidden social conflicts as much as it is a prescription for individual emancipation.

Genre as a Formula, Star as a Genre

There is yet another term used in film studies and which is that of the genre. The genre is a form or a formula of the film in which events and characters appear in a repetitive manner and the cinema becomes formulaic. The formula is very important for the movement images, for the formula helps in anticipation much like the dreamers, madmen, prophesiers and witches in Shakespearean drama, who by forecasting events, help create anticipation about the movements that eventually take place. In a typical popular Indian cinema, the star is the genre; the role played by a star would mean the resolution of the narrative according to the persona of the star. Dilip Kumar's films would imply a masochistic sufferance, Amitabh Bachchan would mean a conquest of the world, and Shah Rukh Khan would mean a definite achievement of his goals and so on.

Star as Extension of the Viewer

Marshall Mc Luhan[4] calls the media as an extension of man; man being used as a gender neutral term. He says that technology that infuses much of the media is an extension of the human body into that media. By this theory, the movement image in the cinema helps viewers extend themselves. The star helps in the extension of the viewer in cinema. Mc Luhan's thesis is useful in analysing the social appeal of film stars, an appeal which has been perhaps the most difficult and under researched areas of cinema studies.

But how does one classify stars, how do we define a star persona as a generic term, a star, and describe the particular instances of stars such as who is Rajesh Khanna, who would be Amitabh Bachchan, or who is Salman Khan? We have yet another problem, how to speak of stars in the growth trajectories of their personas, at which point of do they peak, why do they lose their appeal? We have two questions; firstly, how do we define a star and secondly, how do we think of a star's journey, for a star is a movement image; how do we conceptualise the image in movement?

4 Marshall Mc Luhan. Understanding the Media- Extensions of Man. xxx. 1964. Pg 7

The Star as the Individual : Action

On 17th March 2017, the Delhi Times published a statement of the Indian film actor Govinda, in which he says that there is a hero hidden in every viewer and the fan sees her own image in the star she likes. The premise of my theory of the popularity of the star is exactly as Govinda states; the politics of the personal, or the politics of the personality or of personhood. The discussions around film stars are then necessarily discourses around personhood. Personhood is a modern idea, for without a sense of individualism, personality cannot be relevant. The cinema too is a modern form of art, or entertainment, and hence its alignment with the individual is just perfect; the cinema is a set of moving images, images which are in the process of moving, or in the act of moving, not having wholly moved as yet, but on the anvil of completing movement. The star is, thus, the individual in the process of movement, moving to fulfill her goals, moving away from her constraints, and in this movement, she gathers experiences, wisdom, and insight, and emerges into a personhood that carries with it a greater variety of attributes than what she started off with. The star is the outward representation of the inner movement of individuals in a society; stardom is self-evolution, self-growth. To construct the star as an image that towers over the viewers in an imposing manner is to perhaps make a mistake. The star is the vanishing point for the fan; it is into the star that the fan inseparably disappears, without a trace of her own personhood.

In the Season 5 of the talk show, Koffee with Karan, Priyanka Chopra says that the West has no idea of the following that the Indian film stars have. I think that in the absence of the church or organised ecclesia in India, which includes the Muslims and the Christians, stars are religion. Stars become the 'Overself' of the viewer, seeing in the star an expression of her own life, her purpose, her goals, and her desires. The star is the vindication of the individual's self-worth, a life lived vicariously, and should the star walk in flesh and blood, it becomes fantastic. The star is therefore the individual; the star emerges from the story of the cinema in a manner in which the individual sees herself engage in her everyday life.

The personality has many facets in an age of individuality. In the age of individuality, the material rewards and social recognitions accrue to individuals, and individuals get to also keep the fruits of their individual efforts. This makes rationality, agency and autonomy important traits of the individual personality. Stars are always successful individuals; they can overcome any hurdle in their path to self-fulfillment; not by miracles or by praying or by magic, but by making sustained efforts in the right direction; hence, they are logical and rational as well as effective and determined. Amitabh Bachchan is a big star because he can win under the most trying situations imaginable. He has an enormous technical sense, and he can fight many strong men all at once, solve old criminal cases, and argue well in self-defense. He is determined to get his goals and is confident because he not only wins, but knows that he can win. And he does this much better than any other star in the world of the Hindi cinema.

Individuals also have scale; there are large frame individuals who think very big and there are small scale individuals. The small scale individuals try and achieve those goals set by the society and the establishment; the large scale individuals challenge the very aims of their present civilization. Large scale individuals look into those factors which seem to have disqualified them from attaining the goals set up by the society. They think that there have been things that have created handicaps for them and they must first overcome their socially imposed disabilities in order to enter the level playing field. Large frame heroes are seen in movies as avenging very old and sometimes even forgotten crimes, punishing fathers, taking on the establishment, critiquing the law, widening the scope of jurisprudence and at the end of it, envisioning a whole new polity. The stories of such films are typically those in which the hero and his family are destroyed and despite this, the hero once again returns to a life of wealth and power.

Apropos to scale is the relationship of the hero to the world at large; how he engages with it and to what extent he imagines that he has the capacity to change it in his own vision. We call this sense of capacity to change the world and to take charge of one's own life as individual agency, the extent of the individual's productive powers. Individuals are different from one another due to differences in their sense of agency; there are philosophers who act upon the world with a sense of wholeness; there are obsessive achievers who must get their way irrespective of how the world is structured for everyone else; there are ascetic and resigned individuals who are dispassionate and distanced while there are emotional individuals who absorb the incompleteness of the world and let it rule over them. A philosophical star would be Amitabh Bachchan, the obsessive achiever would be Shah Rukh Khan, the resigned individual would be perhaps Hrithik Roshan, and the passionate man would be Dilip Kumar.

The individual learns something while being socialised by his/her family and peers, and imbibes some other things by experiencing the world all by him/herself. If the individual reflects the values which were taught to her by her family, then she is said to be well socialised, but when the individual absorbs values from directly experiencing the world, she is said to be autonomous and creative. Amitabh Bachchan, because of the misfortunes the hero faces in the world as a child and because of the shelter of the family that he is deprived of, is a man who grows more by experiencing the world first hand; the star is therefore, more autonomous than perfectly socialised.

The star is an active individual whose activity must transform the world, but in the act of transforming it, the individual must outgrow her limits. The star is a soul, her journey through various movies in her capacity as different characters resemble the journey of souls as perhaps in the tales of Jataka.

Looking at the individual as a star, we engage in a kind of a developmental or a spiritual journey. The star is self-taught, one who learns through experience because s/he must go beyond the ordinary and respond creatively to her/his situation. The star as an individual becomes the repository of both instrumental action as well as of transcendental sublimity; her actions become a world view, a generalised mode of cognition, and of self realisation that can only come after a long engagement with the lived in reality.

The Star as an Individual Emotion

The individual is not all about rationality and instrumental action, for she is a bundle of emotions as well. Emotions arise where action is stalled, will contained and activity disrupted.[1] Emotions may be looked upon as breach in expectations. An important part of rationality is of course the management of emotions. Stars are individuals who are more controlled of their emotions, for they emerge out of the numbness that emotions produce in the body and the way they manage emotions become very important for the case of individual creativity and autonomy.

Emotions produce passivity; action is activity and individuals are combinations of both. We associate emotions with passivity and hence, with the feminine, and action with the masculine. Heroines are supposed to be emotional individuals while the hero is supposed to be action oriented. But there is a danger, for when characters are totally bereft of emotions, they turn into villains and vamps, and this is why, Amitabh Bachchan who often would repress his emotions and become too rational, has often been defined as the anti-hero or the one who looks like a villain despite

1 P.V Simonov. Thwarted Action Needed – Informational Theories of Emotions. International Journal of Comparative Psychology. 5(2). 1991

being the protagonist. Rationality which is devoid of emotions is looked down upon in the Hindi films.

The Indian aesthetics, especially as contained in the *Natyashashtra*, the ancient Sanskrit text on the arts, discerns nine kinds of emotions called as the *rasas*, which suggest that the various kinds of emotions must be in balance. It is not unusual to find that the popular cinema mixes pathos with comedy, anger with the sublime and ecstasy with agony in equal measure. Despite this, films do differ in terms of their overall flavor; for there are comedies and there are tragedies, there are the thrillers and then films that are haunting, and there are action films and tear jerkers. In cinema, which produces the movement image, emotions help flavour the sound, for it is the background score or the songs or both, which carry the emotions of the characters on the screen, into the bodies of the viewers.

Emotions help the viewer develop a bond with the characters on the screen.

Emotions in the era of the individual are distinctly different from those in ages when individualism was not so well developed. Emotions in the epics are mainly honour based, based out of the ecstasy of victory or the humiliation of defeat, paradoxically involving more of the Freudian ego. In the age of the individual, as in the age of the stars, emotions involve higher levels of the souls and pertain to the desires to engage in more meaningful relationships, because industrial societies in which the traditional social structures like the caste were demolished, interpersonal cooperation had to be invoked in order to create the society that one lived in. Emotions accordingly became softer and finer in order to build interpersonal bonds with the others. The stars in popular Hindi films were concerned with spinning off a society with more universality than the ones we inherited from our tradition that had deep wedges of caste, creed and religion.

In Amitabh Bachchan's films, emotions were directed not at building bonds, but in fact at cutting off from the bonds that were intimate and those which were nourishing and nurturing, to emerge into a kind of emotional asceticism in which he could concentrate wholly, on not his reproductive but his productive powers. The emotions in popular cinema overwhelmingly centre around romance, which is a reproductive force, while Amitabh as a the hero focused more on the productive powers for an industrial society, productive powers by which humans could transcend the limits of their social class and ascend to higher social and political powers. Clearly, the emotions panned out in Amitabh's films and in the films with other stars were different.

The passions of Shammi Kapoor, or of Rajesh Khanna or even of Dilip Kumar were directed at promoting the reproductive functions of the society, perhaps a politics that emanated out of the rigidities of traditional social divides that prevented the freer intermixing of humans, and which could help procreate a more open society of intermixed marriages. For Amitabh Bachchan, passions were all about loss of home, loss of loved ones, death of father, separation from mother, conflict with brother and a deeper bond with a male friend and an inability to spare time for romance. These emotions helped isolate the hero, direct him to look within himself, reminding us of David Reisman's 'inner directed' person in his work, *The Lonely Crowd*.[2] Such people are isolated from their social moorings and use their own gut feelings to acquire knowledge and wisdom, values and morals, intellect and philosophy and are highly capable and confident, even though sometimes rigid. Emotions, as the ones Amitabh Bachchan would portray on screen, were very useful for individuals to socially climb above their social class, change the objective conditions of their lives and in this way, were politically charged with anger. The soft tearjerker emotions were of individuals who were trapped in their situations while Amitabh's anger was a call for transforming the emotions into action which could defeat those who stood in his path of achievements.

---

2 David Reisman in collaboration with Reuel Denney and Nathan Glazer. The Lonely Crowd – A Study of the Changing American Character. 13th Reprint. Yale University Press. Massachusetts. 1967. Pg 9

Classification of Stars

We now turn to our task of classification of stars, creating criteria for comparing stars like Raj Kapoor, Dev Anand, Dilip Kumar, and Rajesh Khanna on the one hand, and Shah Rukh Khan, Salman Khan and Hrithik Roshan on the other, with Amitabh Bachchan. The idea of such a comparison is not to create a hierarchy of ranks among the stars, for these stars have existed in various points of time, under different viewing circumstances, and have addressed different psychosocial moods of their audiences. The idea behind such comparison is to differentiate stars from one another in order to understand their respective qualities better, and throw the attributes of the persona into a sharper relief. Each star has enjoyed a travel to a peak of popularity and then faced a crisis in their image when they had become hackneyed and were replaced by newer stars, bringing about fresh bouts of entertainment for the viewers.

Deleuze's Principles of Classification of the Movement Image

Deleuze[1] suggests principles of classification of images in cinema according to the sensory perception of the viewer of the

1 Deleuze bases his theory on the theories of consciousness propounded by Henri Bergson in his seminal work, Creative Evolution. Bergson's Creative Evolution is almost a rewriting of Darwin's Origin of Species in which Bergson insists that consciousness develops in cognitive

movement. The first principle is the classificatory system, which is the relative movement of the protagonist and the milieu. When the image moves much slower with respect to the milieu, we have a perception image in which the protagonist appears to be an observer of the world around him and reacts to it, unable to change things by his action; in other words, the world proves too much for him even though in the end his goodness wins over the evil of the world. This is the *perception image*. The world grows organically in its own logic while the hero is essentially an observer, helpless in controlling the forces that shape him. The other extreme of the perception image is the *action image*, in which the action of the protagonist shapes the world. In between, there is a middle ground, when the actor and the world develops organically and parallel to each other and the actor perceives but is yet to act and in this middle space produces the *affection image*. Affection image is the emotional image that braces stars like Dilip Kumar, Rajesh Khanna, Rajendra Kumar and above all the female protagonists of the Indian mainstream cinema. The affection image is an emotional image, emotions being those which are produced within the body organism of the viewers and the stars when the momentum for action is created and yet just stalled at the anvil of movement by resistance.

Raj Kapoor's Perception Image Versus Amitabh Bachchan's Action Image

Every image is a mix of perception, affection and action and each have their own moments of popularity. Raj Kapoor's image is principally a perception image; he is an observer of his surroundings, he remains at the periphery of the frame and looks at the hectic activity around him. He is often seen gazing at the

---

response to the movements of external object beyond the body. Deleuze uses this principle to say that the cinema is therefore a set of movements which develops consciousness in humans by the fact of the movement rather than specifically by what moves. See Gilles Deleuze. Cinema 1 – The Movement Image. First South Asian Edition. Routledge. Continuum. London. 2005. Pg 11.

frame, just as a viewer would do, and through his gaze, we see the beauty of the cloud scalloped skies, the distant villages, the community around him, the rich men and the poor men who pass almost through him, his dreams are elaborate and detailed, he appreciates women and around him, the world goes on in a spin, carrying the viewer with him into the frame. Raj Kapoor is Chaplenisque because the spin of the world carries him and any movement from within him upon the whirlwind of the world becomes a cartoon. The hero played by Raj Kapoor carries a good sense within him, but his refined sensibilities and high ethics remain within him, unable to find space in a world outside driven by greed, lust and meanness; the hero's goodness cannot emerge as a creative force. He is more often than not smothered by the world and gets blown away into its centre as a bag snatcher or a scamster, but eventually returns anchored by beautiful women, mostly played by Nargis[2]. The milieu of the hero collides with him as it does with his viewer and he steps aside to sing his wonderful numbers that are more often commentaries on the world such as *"Main Awara Hoon", "Ichak Daana Beechak Daana"*, or *"Dil ki Baat Sune Dilwallah"*[3]. The hero's central tendency is to find shelter in his moral, ethical, virtuous woman, mostly dressed in white.

When we consider Amitabh Bachchan within the frames of say *Deewar*,[4] we see an action image, an image that drives the milieu, an image and not the world around him that constitutes the rhythm of the movement of the film. Songs are paced not upon the world but are extensions of the hero's bodily movements. The situations are no longer organic but emanate from the thoughts, observations, strategies and reflections. The hero observes, but now through the close up, his face darkens upon us, his features

2 Raj Kapoor's and Nargis' films together are Awara, 1951, Aah, 1953, Shree 420, 1955 and Jaagte Raho, 1956 among the most famous ones.

3 *Main Awara Hoon* is a song from Awara, 1951. *Ichak Dana Bichak Dana* is also from Awara and *Dil ki Baat* is from Shree 420.

4 Deewar, 1975 directed by Yash Chopra, written by Salim Javed, music by R D Burman, co-stars Shashi Kapoor, Nirupa Roy and Parveen Babi and is considered to be the basic text of Amitabh Bachchan.

are very still, his body often freezes on the frame as if a lull before a storm, and then he spins into action; hitting, beating, punching and boxing to pulp his detractors as if through such blows he wants to break out of the frames of his films. Amitabh helps the high morals which Raj Kapoor had held within him to emerge and create the world anew, instead of being smothered by it. Amitabh's image is one of irreverence while Raj Kapoor's is more of helplessness.

Dilip Kumar's Affection Image Versus Amitabh Bachchan's Action Image

We move on to Dilip Kumar's image and let us position ourselves in *Devdas*,[5] for that is the film where the stardom of the thespian congeals and peaks. The hero, unable to get the love of his life withdraws from the world, allows his milieu to grow organically around him while he grows in parallel alongside in yet another organic helix within his sorrows. He lets his sorrow develop in a spiral, the milieu develops in concentric circles around him, and the two motions constitute the melody and the rhythm of the songs of the film. His image is privileged, its movement gets a boost when its own spiral movement is placed against that of a widening world, especially since he moves from the village to the city and then back into the city's extended spaces namely Chandramukhi and Chunnilal's world and then into Paro's life, and eventually in the train and the stage coach to meet both Paro and his own death. Javed Akhtar says of Dilip Kumar that he was capable of a strange stillness[6] and perhaps this would intensify his movement, especially when he would stand against the world as its critic. Dilip Kumar's critic of the world was not one of pathos of Raj Kapoor or of anger of Amitabh Bachchan, but one of banishing the world if it did not measure up to his standards.

---

5 Devdas 1957 directed by Bimal Roy with Suchitra Sen as Paro and Vaijayantimala as Chandramukhi.

6 Javed Akhtar in his talk show *Jaane Pehchaane* on Epic Channel. Season 2. Episode 4. https://www.youtube.com/watch?v=qOuiKuT_lAo

This gives the image an arrogance, a snobbery and heaviness of self-dignity.

Amitabh engages with the world; though reticent and reflective, meditative and mindful, the hero looks upon the world as a work place in which he is the tool to carve out a picture of his own making. Yet, the image which he creates is not a figment of his own imagination but a logical resolution for a fragmentary and conflictual milieu. The paradox of Amitabh's image lies in the fact that by himself he has no need to deal with the world, but emerges upon it in as a task, carried out with a degree of impersonal professionalism. This is why the role of a doctor suited him so well in *Anand*.[7] Amitabh is not born into a situation, for nothing around him can claim his attention; he will rise to the occasion only when he feels the situation needs to be corrected; he has also the distanced engagement of a judge. In Amitabh's films, it is only the hero who acts upon the milieu. The milieu is largely given, it is hopeless and desperate in its oppression of people and the hero steps upon it to punish it, sentence it and even execute it. Amitabh has done well in the role of a lawyer, a policeman, a doctor, a construction engineer, and even a poet, but perhaps never in the role of a painter, because of his impersonality and detachment and very surgical approach.

Dev Anand's Action Image of Small Frame Versus Amitabh Bachchan's Action Image of Large Frame

Using the framework of Deleuze, we may say that Raj Kapoor resembles the perception image, Dilip Kumar the affect image, and Amitabh Bachchan the action image. What about Dev Anand?

? Dev Anand too is an action image and interestingly, by Javed Akhtar's admission, Salim Javed were fans of Dev Anand[8], and in

---

7 Anand, 1969 directed by Hrishikesh Mukherji starring Rajesh Khanna and music by Salil Choudhury. This was the film which is said to have made Amitabh's face recognisable for the first time to the people.

8 Javed Akhtar on Dev Anand in Jaane Pehchaane, aired on Epic Television. Season 2. Episode 3. https://www.youtube.com/watch?v=gbxiY2ZzmSw

fact imagined him as the hero of *Zanjeer*,[9] the film that established Amitabh as the angry young man. But to think about Dev Anand, one has to probe deeper into Deleuze's schema of the action hero in which he further divides the action hero into one with a large frame and the other with a small frame.[10]

The large frame action heroes are those who observe and experience the milieu and action emanates as an activity which is needed to correct the world. Action here changes the situation from S1 to S2; it is a world changing action and hence Deleuze calls it to be of a global frame. This is a S1-A-S2 formula, in which the S1 and S2 are the situations and A is the action. But there is yet another model of action in which the hero acts upon a situation out of his habits, dispositions and the overall innate attitude towards the world, and through such action, he does bring upon a change in the situation, but which gives him an even greater scope for newer action. Deleuze says that this is a small frame of action and uses the formula, A1-S-A2 to describe this. A1 and A2 are actions while S is the situation. We may follow Dev Anand in this frame of action through the film *Kala Pani*[11] in which he takes up a mission of proving his father innocent of a murder which has sent him into prison for life. The opening scene of the film focusses on the hero, depressed and frustrated to near insanity but as he goes out into the world, in search of clues, he is clever, witty, sarcastic and sometimes light hearted and cheerful. He is a man on mission in his various appearances on screen, but he does not have the obsession of holding on to a mental disturbance through each of his actions as Amitabh did in *Zanjeer*, in which the hero holds a hoary memory of the murder of his parents.

---

9 Zanjeer, 1974 was the film that established Amitabh Bachchan as the angry young man. The film was written by Salim Javed, directed by Prakash Mehra, music director Kalyanji Anandji and co-star, Jaya Bhaduri, Ajit and Bindu.

10 See Gilles Deleuze. Cinema 1 – The Movement Image. First South Asian Edition. Routledge. Continuum. London. 2005. Pg 145 and 165.

11 Kala Paani, 1957. Directed by Raj Khosla, Produced by Dev Anand, Navketan Films.

D.P Mukherjee's Principles of Classification of Personalities: Integration of Traits and Balance among Virtues

There is yet another possibility of classification using D.P Mukherjee's idea of the personality and here, one would consider the levels of integration between the various levels of individual responses to the lived-in world[12]. The classification here would be one of degree of integration of the persona, often brought forth through the single mindedness of the star in the pursuit of his or her goals. In simpler terms, we discuss how focused the character is, how much of single-minded concentration s/he can bring into her/his activities. This point is pertinent because the popular cinema upholds the Indian ethos of a balanced personality, which is the perfect mix of duty and pleasure. The problem with Indian cinema is not so much about achieving a balanced personality for its protagonists as much as it is to balance between the demands of being a householder on the one hand and an achiever of goals on the other. Interestingly, the Indian cinema has rarely ever made films on outstanding individuals and it is only now that biopics on sports persons are being made with films like Mary Kom, M.S.Dhoni, Dangal and presently Sachin.

On the one hand, the hero is expected to have superhuman powers of fighting, be a wizard in dancing, a super singer and yet he must sink into the corner of his home to be comforted by parents, siblings, spouse and children. Family, marriage and inheritance remain the foundational structure of mainstream Indian cinema and even when the hero slays the giants, flays the villains, all that he eventually does is to return home. The balance between the achiever and the mediocre, the superhuman and the ordinary person, the pilgrim and the domesticated and the ascetic and the householder is yet another principle along which we can classify our heroes.

---

12 D.P. Mukherjee. Personality and the Social Sciences. Rupa. Delhi. 2004. Pg 19.

Centredness of Superstars

We return to Dev Anand once again. In an attempt to show as many activities as is possible on screen, taking the image through a series of transformations, the problem that Dev Anand faced was indeed one of integration among the variety of faces he showed. The above point can be clearly understood should we imagine Dev Anand in the role of Amitabh Bachchan in *Zanjeer*, just the way it was supposed to be, as planned by Salim Javed, the writers of the film. Amitabh is an integrated persona; while he travels through a variety of situations, each of these get accumulated into his single-minded obsession around the bad dream in which he sees a killer horse. The scare of the nightmare guides him through the waking hours as well, and this perhaps compromises on songs and dances, but the hangover of the fearsome dreams give him a centredness. Superstars assume a heightened level of centredness.

Shah Rukh Khan who is one of the holy trinity of the Khans, played the role of an obsessive lover in *Darr* and *Anjam* and an obsessive avenger of his family in *Baazigar*. *In Dilwale Dulhaniya Le Jayenge*, a cult film of Bollywood, Shah Rukh places his obsessive love for the heroine within the iron frame of the Indian traditions, namely that of marriages which are arranged by parents, to strengthen bonds of alliances between families rather than as a romantic union between two individuals in love with each other. The hemming in of an obsessive love in which a determined lover is all set to marry the girl he loves despite the fact that she has been betrothed to someone else and that too with the approval of the girl's family and rituals of arranged marriage performed duly raises the image of Shah Rukh Khan into an action image. The action image becomes large frame because the action is born out of a constraining milieu and would cease only when the hero affects a complete change if not a reversal of the situation.

Principles of Classification : Relatedness of Stars to Self, Others and The World

We have thus spoken on two classificatory principles; one being the movement image and the other being the integration of personality. Deleuze speaks of the first while D.P speaks of the latter, and we integrate the two for our purpose. There is yet a third principle of classification and this is namely the relatedness of the star to herself, to others and to the impersonal world at large.

First Aspect: Hero's Relatedness to Self

In a typical Indian film, the protagonist faces a situation that threatens to unsettle her from her equilibrium; she is then activated into bringing her life back to this equilibrium. In this unsettlement, her sense of self is jeopardised and she encounters what we might want to call as the non-self. Raj Kapoor fragments in each frame of *Shree 420* when his gold medal holds no value in a city, his degree does not help him find a job and his honesty leaves him homeless and poor. He reverses his poverty and gets rich by compromising everything that he stood for; his complete transformation into his 'non-self' helps him to survive physically, though he is devastated psychologically having lost the love of his life and now almost blackmailed to appease a vampish woman with lust and greed. The hero then returns to his self by demolishing the wealth that he became a part of and returning once more to his poverty, but now with his love with him and the promise that they will fight it out together. Nargis, Raj Kapoor's near mythical heroine, completes the self of the hero, while his action to overcome poverty casts him into his non-self. Raj Kapoor loses his self to his non-self when he acts to overcome a situation and recovers his self only when he returns to the position before his action, albeit with the addition of his romantic interest. Nargis, thus, becomes the end of the act state for Raj Kapoor's image and she is the only legitimate gain which the hero has at the end of a long journey. No wonder Nargis validates Raj Kapoor's action; she helps him regain his lost soul once more, within the parameters of a legitimate world.

How do we see Amitabh Bachchan in *Deewar*? He loses his entity with the loss of his father. But he neither loses his values, nor his reason, attachments or emotions, or the sense of right or wrong. He merely loses his material entitlements. His self-image in fact gets a boost when engaged in a crisis, for here he will draw upon his energies to face the world. At the end of the struggle, the hero does not return to his pristine state; instead, he overcomes and overpowers a hostile world to emerge into a wholesome persona. The hero played by Amitabh Bachchan attains his selfhood only after his long struggle from which he rises as the victor. Success is his self and not his pristineness, and in that success, he does not need a lover or a friend, or for that matter, any approval from any quarter. He is self-appraised, self-certified. The need for success makes the hero into a person who is so autonomous that he can exist as a loner; he really needs no one with him, his world may well be unpeopled. As the cinematic image, this helps in his superstardom for it is only his image which is seen while the rest of the film montage and the other characters are reduced to stereotyped stock material. The hero, in a way is free of any preconceived notion of the self and is open to absorb within his persona an array of capabilities and powers free of any previous entitlements or legacies. His freedom from relationships makes him available for a whole-hearted engagement into the objective reality, just as a scientist would do.

Third Aspect: Hero's Relatedness to the World

In the third aspect of the hero, we mark out his relationship with the world and here we encounter his sense of agency, namely his power to change the world. There are heroes who do not wish to change the world; they would only want to return to their equilibrium. Shah Rukh Khan merely wants to marry the girl he loves in *Dilwale Dulhaniya Le Jayenge* or even in *Darr* or *Anjam*, though the journey which the hero undertakes is not short. But in *Deewar*, the hero played by Amitabh Bachchan questions the paradoxes of law, wants to change the spirit of jurisprudence. Amitabh fights the police and sometimes fights with villains in his capacity of a policeman. Amitabh's existence is bordered by law, the prison, the sentence, the execution, the punishment and assassination, the limits of existence as bounded by physical, legal, institutional, intellectual and even cognitive possibilities.

Second Aspect: Hero's Relatedness to Others

We now come to the second aspect of the hero's relatedness to others in his social milieu. Raj Kapoor finds his identity in the woman he loves, Shah Rukh Khan finds redemption in winning a girl almost as a game. Dilip Kumar evolves in his loss of his love. Amitabh is strangely indifferent to romantic love, indifferent precisely because he has no predefined idea of a self, his selfhood is not attached to anything or anyone, and it only comes into existence during times of overcoming. In terms of Deleuze's movement image, Amitabh Bachchan alone is the quintessential moving image.

During the decades when Amitabh Bachchan was supposed to have been ranked from 1 to 10, Mithun Chakravarty also ran parallel to the hero in the small towns and the villages, those which constituted the periphery of metropolitan India. He too, like Amitabh, was a great fighter, one whose identity emerged from what he would overcome and overpower and not what was intrinsic and essential to him. Like Amitabh, Mithun's existence also centered on the question of oppression by the State; marginalisation by law. The hero too rose to challenge systems, overpower villains who the establishment engendered and sustained. Many chose to call Mithun the poor man's Amitabh Bachchan. But Mithun and Amitabh had a major difference and which was in the way they related to the 'others'. Amitabh's image is that of a loner, a loner because of his autonomy, his ability to stay aloof despite his violent engagement with the world. Mithun is a family person; his world is not one of abstract ideas and conceptual orders, but of concrete and palpable attachments with his kith and kin. Mithun's is an image in which the second criteria comes out very strong and he is deeply embedded within his family rather than bearing a cold and distant relationship of duty towards them.

Classification of Heroines

The Female Centredness of the Popular Hindi Film

The Indian mainstream cinema before Independence was dominated by the lead heroines rather than the male protagonists. The hero would often be a facilitator of a heroine and it were the pains and angst, the joys and satisfaction of the female lead roles that would constitute the crux of the narrative. The rise of the heroes in post-Independent India perhaps runs parallel to the growing masculinisation of the Indian society, its economy and polity and hence, its cinema. Kannan Devi, Devika Rani, Durga Khote, Shanta Apte before Independence and Madhubala, Nargis, Nutan, Meena Kumari, Hema Malini, to mention a few, after Independence, have defined cinema and drawn crowds, irrespective of who the male lead actor has been. However, the portrayal of women on screen has not been very different from the role expectations that the society makes of women in general. Women characters have been glorified as pristine, loyal, heroic in love, committed in relationships, capable of sacrifice and have been lauded for their capacities to bear pain. Paradoxical as it may seem, the world of Bollywood that never breaches the stereotype that women are supposed to be passive and not exercise their agency in taking their lives in the command, still aims to maintain the purity of the feminine. Bollywood, for a very long time, perhaps till the emergence of

Amitabh Bachchan, considered the feminine principle to be constitutive of the society.

Reconciling Women as Movement Images with Their Innate Passivity

Women do not go out and do things; things get done unto them and yet, in cinema, they must be movement images, for the cinema can only have movement images. This is why they constitute the affection image; emotions swell when action is prevented. However, not all women are passive; we have a Hema Malini in *Seeta Aur Geeta* and a Rekha in *Khoon Bhari Maang* who are veritable action masters performing stunts and fights. The huge commercial success of these films show that women need not have been turned into passive actors with only tears to shed. Unfortunately, women in Indian cinema have been confined to their social roles, and perhaps only a possible way of classifying them is by the kind of obstacles they face in achieving their love. Interestingly, in *Seeta Aur Geeta* as well as in *Khoon Bhari Maang*, the goals of the women lead actors were not to get their lovers, but to set a wrong world right. If we do not waiver from Deleuze's principle of the movement image, heroines become the affection image as they encounter situations against which they must move, but are trapped into inactivity by the social stereotypical roles assigned to them; the stalled actions are reasons for their emotions. Heroines, thus, are classified also by the kind of stress they face in prevailing in their self-hood; their selves are constantly threatened and challenged.

Principles of Classification of Heroines: The Nature of Stress Faced by Affection Images

In *Saheb Bibi aur Ghulam* or *Pakeezah*, and even in a relatively small scale production, *Dil Ek Mandir*, Meena Kumari plays the role of a heroine who is torn between her traditional role of a wife or even a prostitute and a romantic lover, the latter being free of encumbrances of social roles. Meena Kumari is pulled in two directions, one to conform and the other to transgress the ties that bind her. Here the stress is between her passions and duties, between her state of being a prostitute and that of a wife. Nothing shows the stress between the prostitute and the wife better than the rendition of the song, "Na Jao Saiyan". In *Saheb Bibi aur Ghulam* in which she dresses up as a prostitute to entice her husband to stay the night with her instead of the brothel appears to be a signature of the heroine's image.

Nutan, yet another celebrated heroines of Hindi cinema, is seen at the margins of life; she is either in prison on charges of murder in *Bandini*, or thrown out of her foster family on account of her caste in *Sujata*, and even in a much later film, *Saudagar*, her husband abandons her in his pursuit of a younger woman.

Sharmila Tagore frequently lost her lover and rediscovered him under changed appearances; in *Talaash* she herself undergoes the change in appearance and in *Aradhana*, her lover returns to her in the appearance of her son. The selfhood prevails across changes in her situation and this constitutes the distinctive character of her image.

The woman is supposed to respond in standard ways of emotional attachments to her family and her lover. The villain separates the body and the soul of the heroine, casting her image into a tragedy brought about due to this separation. Only her deep attachment to her family returns her to her torn selfhood, torn because of the separation of the body and soul. It is through her love for others that she reunites and integrates herself. The heroine is an epitome of virtue and never does she waver in her dedication to her marriage; she may meet her old lover as in *Kabhie Kabhie* or in *Dil Ek Mandir Hai*, but there is no question for her to step outside of her marriage. For vices, there is the vamp who tempts the hero out of the heroine and hence she is a threat to the good woman. Women actors are not supposed to engage to change the world and they do not do so either.

How Women Privilege Movement

Cinema has much to gain when the main movement image is the heroine. For one, heroine-centred films tend to create parallel movements, in the image and in the milieu and the balancing act of two distinct movements gives rise to wonderful rhythms expressed in melodious music and mellifluous lyrics. Nature figures better in female-led films with evocative metaphors. Socially, the heroine-led films are more argumentative with greater intellectual stimulation for its viewers. Resolutions of narratives are less certain; films have more scope for interpretation. Mature societies often have female-led films while societies where arguments seem to surrender to already made up minds and hardened opinions tend to swing towards the more male-oriented cinema, usually of action.

Heroines of the Amitabh Era: Various Forms of Passivity

It is said that Amitabh Bachchan brought about a great transformation in the flavour of the Hindi film by changing over to the masculine from the feminine. The cinema as a medium proliferated also perhaps due to this reason, as cinema halls mushroomed all over the country and its appeal went beyond the matinee hours of housewives and college girls. The quality of music, according to most, also deteriorated, and the quality of film experience changed from the relaxed entertainment to chair-clutching high-paced thrill. Movement shifted from the feminine to the masculine, from the affect to action, but most importantly, from stress to violent conflict. The heroine was more or less redundant in times of Amitabh Bachchan and thrived mainly as a stereotyped construct designed to elicit male sexual gaze upon her body and the distinction between the vamp and the heroine collapsed. Actresses like Zeenat Aman and Parveen Babi, who in the earlier years would have perhaps been vamps, with their revealing clothes and wanton ways, now became the hero's love interest; the woman as the epitome of virtue was made redundant because women were no longer considered as humans, but were in fact considered tools for the satisfaction of the male desire. The so-called virtuous feminine was protected through Rakhee, Rekha and Jaya Bhaduri.

Rakhee was a heroine who had all the assumed values that women were supposed to have; nurturing, placid, obedient, submissive and yet capable of assertion and revenge if the need arose like in *Shraddhanjali*. Rakhee was gorgeous to look at in a traditional way and she held all the attributes of femininity in such balanced and equal proportions that she was really left without any defining characteristics. Perhaps, this is why she was cast as the detective in a film based on Agatha Christie's Miss Marple, in Rituparno Ghosh's film, *Shubho Mahurat*. She was the virtuous woman all through and no one saw this better than Gulzar, her husband, when he wrote *Baseraa*, with Shashi Kapoor as the hero in which she gives up her husband for her livelier younger sister, played by Rekha. Rakhee is quick to sacrifice for the more vital sexuality of younger men and women, and no wonder, the film *Tapasya* had her in the lead role as a natural choice. In *Kabhie Kabhie* she gives up her claim on Amitabh Bachchan without a cry and in *Kasme Vaade*, in yet another role opposite Amitabh Bachchan, she banishes her own desires when she loses her fiancé in a shoot-out and refuses to warm up to his look alike who wants to love her. Interestingly, this passive femininity of Rakhee takes on shades of violence *in Muqaddar Ka Sikandar* when her utter ordinariness makes her incapable of empathy towards the love of Sikandar for her.

Jaya Bhaduri Bachchan is perhaps the least passive of Amitabh's heroines, for she, like Amitabh, is more concerned about finding her own centre in life and for which she undergoes deep transformations. She transforms from a school girl in utter adulation for a film star to a coy young woman in love with a normal young man in *Guddi*, from a carefree person to an emotionally ruined woman in *Abhiman*, from a naïve and a trusting student to eloping with a lover in *Chupke Chupke*. Jaya has been perhaps the most active of all heroines in the age of Amitabh. Her image required that scripts be written for her but during Amitabh's era, scripts were created only for the action hero, leaving Jaya out of the reckoning for most producers. Jaya and Amitabh's marriage has endured over 40 years now, and each has maintained His and her identity within the marriage much like in their films together.

Rekha is the most adored woman among Amitabh's heroines. She is somewhere in between the passivity of Rakhee and a prospect of having her own identity as Jaya. Her identity is her promise which her image suppresses under the utter ordinariness of the feminine attributes; Rekha is always at the anvil; she forces herself to appear as non-ambitious and coy while at the same time having the capacity to fight tigers all by herself as in *Khoon Pasina and Mr Natwarlal*. Rekha complements Amitabh as a partner in a duet, while Raakhee and Jaya need Amitabh to play along as an accompanist.

Writers as Shadow Directors

The inventor of the image of Amitabh Bachchan is of course, without even a shred of doubt, the writer duo, Salim Javed. These writers invented a form of the Hindi popular cinema into which Amitabh Bachchan fitted in aptly. This form is the discovery of action, or of the action image. Salim Javed started their career variously but came to converge as resident writers in G.P.Sippy's production under which they wrote films like *Andaz*, *Seeta Aur Geeta* and *Haathi Mere Saathi*. They wrote *Sholay* and *Shaan* as well, but by then, they had struck out as independent individuals, known to the world as writers. Before *Zanjeer*, produced by Trimurti Films, Salim and Javed were as invisible as any writer in the Hindi film industry. Writers, particularly, were not given any acknowledgment and they almost never received any credit in the films. They were also paid less. Salim Javed not only became legendary in claiming credit in film titles but became a major draw for films written by them. Soon they claimed fees higher than those of the stars. Dialogues along with songs of *Sholay* and *Zanjeer* would be played on Vividh Bharati, and the film industry where Lata Mangeshkar fought for the inclusion of the playback singer's name, actually granted Salim Javed their space. This was because of the innovation they brought into the Hindi film, and that innovation was action.

Biographically, the three young men, Salim Khan, Javed Akhtar and Amitabh Bachchan were similarly placed at their respective moments of life when they met. All were trying to make it out in the world on their own and had rather different childhood experiences, which nonetheless, converged into what came out in their projects together. Salim Khan lost his parents early in life but lost his mother earlier, only at the age of nine. Since she died of tuberculosis, he was not allowed to be near her as far as he remembers. He lost his father just as he was about to enter college. Javed Akhtar lost his mother Safiya Akhtar, a woman of talent and substance, a poet and a teacher, and was hurt when his father Janissar Akhtar remarried. His father was an eminent Urdu poet and a song writer and Javed Akhtar's turning away from lyrics into film scripts was perhaps a way of dissociating himself from his father. He found a father figure in Kaifi Azmi, another Urdu poet and a Hindi film lyricist of eminence, whose daughter, Shabana Azmi, he eventually married. These biographical episodes are reflected in the stories they wrote.[1]

Amitabh Bachchan's childhood is normal middle class but with caveats; his father was an eminent poet, a faculty of English literature at the Allahabad University and his mother worked as a teacher at the DAV school. A Sikh by birth, Teji Bachchan was ambitious and liberal minded. It was she who planned that Amitabh and his younger brother have the best of education, and her husband should be well-connected with people in high places. Amitabh's career choice to enter the corporate world in Kolkata came from his preference for the fast city, neon lights, parties and socialisation. He had a point to prove to his mother and his moving away from his father's profession of fame into his mother's choice of financial success shows that it was to his mother that he showed a greater allegiance.

---

1 The Wikipeadia has been consulted for biographies of Salim Khan and Javed Akhtar. For Amitabh Bachchan's biography, Soumya Bandopadhyay's Amitabh Bachchan (Bengali) has been referred to, published by, Ananda Publishers, Kolkata.1995.

The biographies of the three men, in one way or the other, centre around a missing father and an overwhelming mother. These themes occurred throughout Amitabh's films with Salim Javed.

Amitabh's image was a convergence of three aspects of the hero's onscreen biography; one was against the unjust social institutions which debarred people from participating in and contributing towards the development of the society. The second aspect was the hero's desire to step into his father's shoes because the father failed him while the third was his deep attachment for his mother, who he could go to any extent for to make her comfortable in life.

Manmohan Desai was perhaps the final sailing away point for Amitabh because after the runaway success of *Amar Akbar Anthony*, each said of the other that they would forever make films with each other. Amitabh appears to have been fonder of Manmohan Desai than of Salim Javed; possible that the angry image was tiring him out a bit. Salim Javed also seemed to compete with Amitabh Bachchan, sometimes bargaining for higher fees than the star and they did get it; Amitabh may have been competitive as well, for, he wanted to prove that the star was bigger than the writer[2].

Don in 1978 may have been the final claim for credit of the image; Salim Javed integrated the two faces of Amitabh; one, the ruthless and somber figure, wholly in command of the world and the other, a relaxed and spontaneous street performer, at the nadir of the power structure of that world. It is interesting that Salim Javed would give a hierarchy to the two images, placing the angry hero in a higher status than the more joyous Anthony Gonsalves kind of creation of Manmohan Desai. There is a competition between the two images and the competitive tone of the film came out very well, perhaps because of the competition between Amitabh Bachchan and Salim Javed.

---

2 Diptakirti Chaudhuri. Written By Salim- Javed. Penguin. Delhi. 2015. Pg 283.

Despite *Sholay* and *Immaan Dharam*, Salim Javed was not as comfortable as Manmohan Desai in working with multi-starrers. Multi-starrers needed a different kind of understanding of cinema than what Salim Javed was good at.

The essence of the writer duo was reinterpretation; *Deewar* had shades of *Ganga Jumna* and *Mother India* and even of *Mughal-e-Azam*, when the father and son talk to each other on the anvil of the internecine war that they are about to wage at each other. *Kabhie Kabhie*, *Deewar* and *Trishul* had clutches of material lifted from Manoj Kumar's *Roti Kapdaa Aur Makaan*.

Discourses from these films were deconstructed, power dimensions rediscovered, ideologies contested and then the stories were twisted with a new sense of politics of entitlement. Amitabh Bachchan was thus positioned to question the old cinema classics, and in this way, was made to look like a rebel who stood against the old system of thought, beliefs, orientations and of course, cinema making. Manoj Kumar was the good man turned into a criminal in order to educate his brothers and marry his sister off in *Roti Kapdaa Aur Makaan*. In the film, the hero squarely blames his unemployment for his ills; in *Deewar*, the film that made Amitabh Bachchan into the star that he became, the hero blames the establishment, its institutions, its laws and its discourses for the social ills. The entire frame of the cinema is elevated from the personal in *Roti Kapdaa Aur Makaan* to the generic in *Deewar*. Salim Javed must be credited for changing the scale of cinema.

Salim Javed invented the image of the angry young man and with that also changed the formula, the montage and the feel of the popular cinema, taking it away from within the reach of the urbanised middle classes to the marginalised masses, from discourses of tradition and modernity to the arguments against law, ethics, State and citizenship. Salim Javed made Amitabh Bachchan into a formula unto himself, and into the formula of Hindi films since then. The three together imbibed the tone of the new politics of Mrs Gandhi, one that moved away from the Nehruvian politics of modernising India from a traditional country into an India that was looking for upward social mobility for its newly-emerging lower- middle classes into positions previously held by only the entrenched elites.

What is more interesting is that it was not before *Hum Aaapke Hain Kaun* and *Dilwale Dulhaniya Le Jayenge* in 1993 and 1994respectively that the Hindi film returned to the middle classes once again; however, with new concerns of sexuality in which the men were less confident and women less shy. With the coming of the multiplexes post-1996, and the complete transformation of the Hindi popular cinema, the cinema changed from its previous form that addressed a life as universally lived and experienced, to slices of life experienced uniquely in interesting situations. The situation became important; the star less so.

Prakash Mehra versus Manmohan Desai

Prakash Mehra was the director who midwifed the angry young image of Amitabh Bachchan in 1974 in *Zanjeer*. He then invented Amitabh's comic role in *Hera Pheri* two years later in 1976. But it seems that from *Hera Pheri*, Manmohan Desai took over Amitabh Bachchan when he cast the star in *Amar Akbar Anthony*, discovering in him the capability of side-splitting comedy.

Salim Javed's angry hero, a sterling discovery of the Hindi cinema and as the hero of *Zanjeer* and *Deewar*, *Trishul* and *Kala Paththar*, Amitabh would have scaled heights of the Hindi cinema, but perhaps never been the megastar he was without Manmohan Desai.For a man who is at war with the world may be a revolutionary, but he is lonely, and as George Lukacs says that such a man may have peers among the stars in the sky, but never an earthly companion.[1] Manmohan Desai's Amitabh returns to the earth from his home in the yonder, accepts the imperfections of the world rather than seek the perfections in the Beyond, and is existentialist rather than a metaphysist; a pragmatic rather than an idealist. The order of the release of the films was important

1 George Lukacs. Theory of the Novel. 1962. Reprinted by Merlin Press. UK. 2003. Pg 45

as well; without the agony of Vijay Verma of *Deewar*, the ecstasy of Anthony Gonsalves would not have had the appeal that it did.

In *Hera Pheri* in 1976, Prakash Mehra tried to break the hermitically sealed seriousness of the hero of *Zanjeer* by introducing some play as well as horseplay into the character of Amitabh Bachchan; this he may have thought was appropriated by Manmohan Desai in *Amar Akbar Anthony*. Prakash Mehra emerged in 1978 with *Muqaddar Ka Sikandar*, with *Lawaaris* in 1981 and *Sharaabi* in 1984, the three constituting a trilogy of sorts. In these, Prakash Mehra moved far away from the hero in *Zanjeer* and created a man attached to this world, to his earthly companions and to the here and now of a contingent life. While in *Muquaddar Ka Sikandar* the hero was an orphan, in *Lawaaris* and *Sharaabi* he was estranged from his father. In *Muquaddar ka Sikandar*, he was self-abnegating, in *Lawaaris*, defiant and in *Sharaabi*, sardonic; in short, the negativity of the hero remained encoded at the core of his character. No wonder then despite huge block busters, Prakash Mehra 's films did not create a signature for Amitabh Bachchan as Manmohan Desai's films did, though *Muqaddar Ka Sikandar* is among one of the most tragic films ever made in the repertoire of Amitabh's filmography.

Manmohan Desai's montage was totally different from that of Prakash Mehra, for his frames had the movement not found so obviously in Prakash Mehra's cinema. *Sharaabi* or *Lawaaris* had the camera almost as steady as in *Zanjeer*. On the other hand, Manmohan Desai's frames moved very fast, giving Amitabh Bachchan a whole new body language. The movement of Desai's camera made way for a new kind of music by Lakshmikant Pyarelal who remained a part of the Manmohan Desai and Amitabh Bachchan projects. When *Dostana* was made in 1980 by Raj Khosla, written by Salim Javed, and starring Amitabh Bachchan and Shatrughan Sinha, the music directors were Lakshmikant Pyarelal. The change in the music meant a change in the movement and in the movement image of Amitabh Bachchan and through Laxmi-Pyare, Manmohan Desai's style got a boost over that of Prakash Mehra.

Manmohan Desai made *Parvarish, Coolie, Naseeb, Suhaag and Desh Premee* but he also made *Mard, Toofan* (directed by Ketan Desai) and *Ganga Jumna Saraswati*. In the last mentioned three films, Manmohan exaggerated the hero's actions, bloated the narratives and seemed to be totally ready to imbibe the sarcasm, the desperation and the self-pity of Prakash Mehra's versions of Amitabh Bachchan. In his mind, Manmohan was most probably envious of Prakash Mehra's clout with Amitabh Bachchan. Both directors were very possessive about Amitabh, both tried to outdo the other and made films in competition with each other, becoming more garish, ostentatious and exhibitionist, and made a narrative out of Amitabh Bachchan's persona.

Manmohan Desai placed Amitabh in a whirlwind of competition and cooperation with other characters; his roles being constantly defined and redefined, his boundaries and spaces being reconstituted over and over again, vis-à-vis the co-stars. For Prakash Mehra, the co-stars were primarily props to uphold the image of Amitabh Bachchan, and hence, his films depended solely on the superstar for its inner momentum and which of course would have to be limited if it is constituted singly by the protagonist.

Yash Chopra, Mukul Anand and Game Changers

Yash Chopra

When at the turn of the millennium, Amitabh Bachan faced a paradox of fate, namely having won the title the Star of the Millennium and falling into an impossible debt trap with the failure of his company, the ABCL, it seems by his own account, that one morning he walked into Yash Chopra's office and asked him for a job.[1] Yash Chopra cast him in a lead role in the film *Mohabbatein* directed by his son, Aditya Chopra, a film based on the Dead Poet's Society, a Peter Weir film, based on a novel by Thomas Schulman and bearing a very close resemblance to Tagore's play, Red Oleanders.[2] This film turned Amitabh Bachchan around and made him 'cast ready' to act in a slew of films that

1 http://indiatoday.intoday.in/story/amitabh-bachchan-ranbir-kapoor-failure-ae-dil-hai-mushkil/1/815944.html

2 Red Oleanders: Rabindranath Tagore. Rakta Larabi (Bengali). Red Oleanders (Translation).Viswa Bharati. Also see the web version. http://www.tagoreweb.in/Render/ShowContent.aspx?ct=Plays&bi=72EE92F5-BE50-40D7-4E6E-0F7410664DA3&ti=72EE92F5-BE50-4FE7-8E6E-0F7410664DA3.

was supposed to start a whole new phase of his life. Yash Chopra no longer directed him nor did Aditya Chopra, but many film makers especially Ram Gopal Varma, Ravi Chopra, Sujoy Ghosh and even Farhan Akhtar 'picked up the stocks' again.

Yash Chopra's *Mohabbatein* was interesting, for it observed that the rebel image of the young Amitabh was somewhere a self-involved and a self-absorbed person who grew perhaps self-righteous and moralistic and became rigid. Indeed, David Reisman in his book, *The Lonely Crowd*, says that the inner directed man, a category that best defines Amitabh Bachchan's roles in films, is one who learns by experience rather than by socialising, and one who turns to himself for his own strength, a self-made man but one who also tends to be rigid, punishing and unyielding.[3] While Yash Chopra had explored the inner directedness of Amitabh in terms of his reflections and meditations, he also explored the rigid side of the hero. We see the first attempts at exploring the inflexibility of the character in *Mohabbatein*. The man who challenged institutions has now, due to the success of his revolution, become the order, perfect and very rigid in that perfection. He builds a world with the high walls of ideals, which exiles the concrete reality, and hence becomes the same hegemonic power that he, in his youth, would attack.

Mohabbatein raised the same paradoxes as *Deewar* would raise, namely the dissociation of the ideals from the lived-in concrete of the reality. In *Deewar*, Amitabh challenged the system by pointing out that the law imposed conditions from above, without considering the context of human actions. But in *Mohabbatein*, he has himself become the system, who now rigidly holds on to his ideas without any regard of how the world changes around him. Yash Chopra created a whole new slot for the hero to be sought after again; those directors who were not fortunate to be around at the time of Amitabh

---

3 David Reisman et al. The Lonely Crowd – A Study of the Changing American Character. The Yale University Press. USA. 1950. Pg 9.

seemed to have got into a new phase of opportunity to work with this legendary figure. Yash Chopra's discovery of Amitabh Bachchan, who could become his own contradiction, was thus a major invention, as big an invention as the angry young man of *Deewar*.

Among all of Amitabh's directors, I would say that Yash Chopra was perhaps the unlikeliest of them all and this is despite the fact that he directed Amitabh in films that should be counted among his best, namely *Deewar*, *Kala Paththar*, *Kabhie Kabhie*, *Trishul* and later *Silsila*. Yash Chopra is a man of romance while Amitabh Bachchan appears to be a cynical man, sardonic and even downright contemptuous of love, lust and conjugality, whether in romance or in marriage. Perhaps this is why Yash Chopra was successful in identifying in Amitabh, a man who purposefully avoids romance, steels his heart to passions, skips his instincts and resolves to engage in only work in order to single-mindedly achieve his goals. One wonders whether a man less romantic than Yash Chopra could have identified this romance-shunning side of Amitabh Bachchan. Usually heroes in Hindi popular cinema treat romance as a routine, the song and dance being the expected thing in the bouquet of entertainment they offer; Amitabh seemed to be an exception to this. Yash Chopra created this exception and in separating romance from Amitabh, further split the image of the hero. In the essays discussing Amitabh's image, we have already mentioned that the split in the hero's image created a certain kind of 'lack' or 'absence' that needed to be filled up. In the Amitabh romances, namely *Kabhie Kabhie* and *Silsila*, the hero wrenches himself out of his desires and emotions and settles into a life of heart-rending tragedy.

There was also another split that Yash Chopra was successful in bringing about in Amitabh Bachchan, but this was more the doing of Salim Javed, which was to create a hero displaced from a life which he deserves, a man who is derailed from his providence, making his life a journey of struggle, of settling scores, of revenge and retribution.

Mukul Anand

Amitabh Bachchan had crashed once before his huge bankruptcy in business in 2000; this was the crashing out that happened with his resignation from politics on accusations of corruption in 1987. He returned to films with Tinnu Anand's *Shahenshah* and *Main Azad Hoon*, Prakash Mehra's *Jadugar* and Manmohan Desai's *Toofan* and *Mard* and *Ganga Jumna Saraswati*, and unfortunately, all failed at the box office. He acted in K.C.Bokadia's *Aaj Ka Arjun* and in Shashi Kapoor's *Ajooba*, which collapsed almost without a trace, as did films like *Insaniyat*, *Kohram*, *Lal Badshah* or *Sooryavansham*, the last mentioned being a forerunner of *Mohabbatein* in many ways. During this time, in the year 1990, Mukul Anand directed the film *Agneepath*. Amitabh subsequently acted in *Hum* and *Khuda Gawah* by the same director. Mukul Anand died young but he was a promising auteur who created a new style around Amitabh Bachchan's image. Amitabh, in Mukul Anand's film, becomes a 'had been', a man now much older and more accepting of the limitations of his action and thought and is more resigned to the challenges to his existence. He is resigned into compromises with life and is seasoned enough not to hone romantic ideas of a revolution. He is a hero who has been there, done that and seen all of it. It was Mukul Anand's genius that saw the Shakespearean Julius Caesar in Amitabh Bachchan in the film *Agneepath*. He explored his homelessness in *Khuda Gawah*, and in *Hum*, he confined the hero in his solitude, deprived both of his love as well as of his heroic life.

Just as Yash Chopra had split Amitabh's image into a man separated from his heart because of his essential separation from a life due to him, Mukul Anand split his image into a past and a present. He gathers all the appearances of Amitabh Bachchan, aggregates them and then pushes them into a corner called the 'past' life of the hero and spices him up anew for the present. The present and the past enter into a relationship of forgetfulness and memory, of resignation and appetence, of relinquish and desiring.

Ram Gopal Varma

Kudos to Ram Gopal Varma for casting Amitabh in *Sarkar* and its sequel. Ram Gopal has been able to abstract out Amitabh's essence, which is action. *Sarkar* is an action film with Amitabh Bachchan as the ageing hero, barely being able to move, confined to his chair, but is nonetheless the action hero. *Sarkar* discovers that Amitabh's action is not about his physical movements, but a trajectory of thought constituted in the mind. *Sarkar* shows action as a logical train of thought; it is a way of logically sewing together events and hence opens up Amitabh for yet another generation of action films and helps place Amitabh once more into the reckoning of heroes. Farhan Akhtar's *Vazir* and Sujoy Ghosh's *Te3n* were similar films which exploited the action image of Amitabh Bachchan despite the hero being an old, bereaved and a physically disabled man between the two films.

Hrishikesh Mukherjee

Perhaps the most talented director that Amitabh got to work with is Hrishikesh Mukherjee. This is because he made quite a star out of Amitabh Bachchan without ever touching the angry chord in him. Amitabh was cast in very different roles in all of Hrishikesh Mukherjee's films; *Anand*, *Namakharam*, *Abhimaan*, *Mili*, *Chupke Chupke*, *Jurmana* and *Bemisal* and despite such different roles and different images, Amitabh becomes a star for the first time in Hrishikesh Mukherjee's films. This is despite the fact that Jyoti Swarup had cast him in *Parwana* from which Salim Javed identified him for their films *Zanjeer* and *Deewar*, Basu Chatterjee cast him in *Manzil* a remake of a Mrinal Sen movie, *Akash Kusum*, Dulal Guha directed Amitabh in *Do Anjaane*, and Sudhendu Roy in *Saudagar*, Ravi Nagaich in *Pyar Ki Kahani* and the star of them all, K.A.Abbas cast Amitabh in *Saat Hindustani* as a debut actor – all these top level directors put together could not create the magic of Hrishikesh Mukherjee, who was able to make a star out of the actor without ever putting him up as a lead actor. For Hrishikesh Mukherjee, Amitabh has always been a supporting cast and never the protagonist.

If we observe closely, then we may discover that in each of Hrishikesh Mukherjee's films, the characters Amitabh played had a major void which needed filling up either by his male co-actor or by his heroine. In no case in a Hrishikesh Mukherjee film was the character played by Amitabh Bachchan complete by himself, never quite self-contained, and instead, carried within him an angst that comes out of not being able to find satisfaction in his existence. In *Anand*, he is uncomfortable with death, in *Namak Haram*, uneasy with a labour union's demand for fair wages, in *Abhimaan*, at his wit's end when his wife does better than him, in *Mili* he is unable to open up to a spontaneous girl, in *Bemisal* he feels out of sorts because he has been showered with a kindness which he cannot repay and in *Jurmana* he suffers from guilt when he seduces a trusting girl, and in all these roles, Amitabh needs to be moderated, tempered, rationalised and even corrected. Hrishikesh Mukherjee's Amitabh Bachchan is therefore a split image as well, a so-called less developed personality with faults forced to encounter situations from which he must evolve, out to reach a higher plane of existence and even wisdom. To understand the personality of the star as merely a problem-solving person, or a character who maintains integrity while overcoming objective impediments, is therefore not so much of an entertainment as a star, like the one Amitabh Bachchan emerged into, a person with fractures forever in a state of inner strife to become into a whole.

I think that it was Jyoti Swarup in his film *Parwana* which was one of Amitabh's earlier films in the industry, who first cast him into a role where a good man consumed by his passions turns into an offender. *Parwana* was not a hit because while the negative hero played by Amitabh was in every sense the hero of the film, the director constantly focused on Navin Nishchol, the good guy. It was as if Yash Chopra were to place Sunny Deol as the hero of *Darr* instead of projecting Shah Rukh Khan. *Parwana* and *Darr* were similar stories of an unrequited or rather an unnoticed lover turning into a villain and is a tricky formula but *Parwana*, despite being less talked of, kickstarted Amitabh's career, just as *Darr* was to be the premise of Shah Rukh Khan as the superstar. *Parwana* raised the expectations around Amitabh Bachchan as a great actor.[1]

---

1 Soumya Bandopadhyay. Amitabh Bachchan (Bengali). Ananda Publishers. Kolkata. 1995. Pp 189-190. and also see https://www.cinestaan.com/articles/2016/mar/3/630/who-was-the-real-hero-in-bombay-to-goa

The Music Directors

Strangely as it seems but truly so, Amitabh Bachchan's era in cinema ended an entire style of film making that went before him. Amitabh's films changed the formula of the cinema in which the hero became vengeful and rather than focus on romance and employment, was more interested in the higher civic duty of correcting the world. Politically, the era of Amitabh Bachchan's cinema emerged in times of a sense of greater agency in the people, a natural outcome of the progress of democracy. I have found it interesting that in none of Amitabh's films except for some fleeting moments in *Khoon Pasina* and *Lawaaris*, the hero never went to ask for a job. Amitabh was always an entrepreneur, generating work by himself, earning through the deployment of his own talents, intelligence and experience.

R. D. Burman and Amitabh Bachchan Misfit

By the 1970's, political protests mainly in the public sector institutions and in organised factories, schools and colleges erupted. These protests extended the human body beyond her physical confines and R. D. Burman's music just did the same. Music does best to capture the bodily movements and no one did it better for the cause of freeing the body as R. D. Burman's music.

R.D. Burman, better referred to as R. D., created a certain school of music, which had two major characteristics; one was that music elicited a response from the gut, hitting at the core of the stomach and then travel up the esophagus to the rib cage, or travelling along the chakras as per a certain branch of philosophy. The use of the empty beat to pitch his rhythm created this kind of a hollow feeling inside the body and had the effect of literally turning the stomach out. The second feature was that the notes were extended out so that the song always seemed to be running behind to catch the tune which seemed to roll out. In short, R. D.'s music extended the body, in the manner in which Mehmood jumps out of the window in *Padosan* or Jaya Bhaduri and Randhir Kapoor move with abandon in *Jawani Diwani* or the manner in which Rajesh Khanna almost floats in *Kati Patang*.

R.D. Burman was the music director in quite a few of Amitabh starrers, *Great Gambler* and *Kasme Vaade* being among the most remembered. Amitabh's montage changed to accommodate R.D.'s musical flares, the background consisted of much larger panorama of open spaces.[1] Ramesh Sippy, the erstwhile employer of Salim Javed, directed *Sholay*, *Satte Pe Satta* and *Shaan*, all of which had R D Burman as the music maker. Interestingly, all of the above mentioned films were made in the background of undulating landscapes in order to make space for the movement of the music.

Amitabh's best films like *Zanjeer*, *Deewar*, *Trishul*, *Amar Akbar Anthony*, *Don*, *Naseeb* and even *Coolie* and *Muquaddar Ka Sikandar* were shot in closed spaces to give his body movements a closer framing. The music of *Great Gambler* and *Kasme Vaade* interestingly did more for the landscapes than brace the action or the bodily rhythm of the hero. Kalyanji Anandji were more successful in exploiting the bodily movements of Amitabh Bachchan. In fact, the film *Don* in which the film grew around its music, the music directors, Kalyanji Anandji were almost the directors of the film as well. Kalyanji Anandji also directed music for Amitabh's first film *Zanjeer* in which though the hero had no song composed on him; the music seemed to surround

1 R D Burman was the music composer for *Deewar*, *Satte Pe Satta*, *The Great Gambler*, *Kasme Vaade*; incidentally all very successful at the box office.

him and sought his innate rhythm that lay repressed beneath deep layers of melancholy. Amitabh's body would take in, churn it in and then channelise the emotions through razor sharp action. R. D.'s music is light bodied because it broods at nothing, Amitabh needs deeper and intense beats to align with his habit of absorbing things within himself.

Don in 1978 is made to reveal Amitabh's bodily rhythm and this is why, music is the master of its montage.[2] The story of *Don*, with Amitabh in two roles, one dead and the other impersonating the dead and continuously trying to match up and catch up with the memories of a dead man, is the essence of the music of this film. It is difficult to remake *Don*, though such attempts have been made with Shah Rukh in the lead and the difficulty arises precisely because no one, but no one in the Hindi film industry has been able to work with a split image as Amitabh has done.

Indeed, in the film, *Satte Pe Satta*, R. D. Burman too tried to incorporate the music of the split image, the split being between a good guy who goes missing and a bad guy who impersonates him. The scene in which Babu, the bad guy keeps a photo of Ravi, the good guy and tries to emerge like him is the crux of both the montage as well as of its music. *Kasme Vaade* with R.D. Burman's music too had a good guy and a bad guy, the good one being the dead one in this case, but because the two were kept separate and out of each other's ways, the music did not need to make that effort to bring together the splits.

Laxmikant Pyarelal set many of Manmohan Desai's films to tune and since after *Amar Akbar Anthony*, almost all of Manmohan Desai's films cast Amitabh Bachchan, one can say that for some time in their career, the music director duo were very much a part of the Amitabh's journey through stardom. But Laxmikant Pyarelal focused more on Manmohan Desai's montage than on the body of Amitabh Bachchan. Manmohan Desai placed Amitabh in multi-starrers with full justice to every other star in the frame, as opposed to Prakash Mehra who would make the

---

2 Krishna Gopalan. The Making of Don. Rupa. Delhi. 2013.

male co-stars subservient to Amitabh Bachchan, casting them as supportive characters. Prakash Mehra's films perhaps needed Kalyanji Anandji who could concentrate only on Amitabh's bodily movements, making the whole film an outcome of the actor's innate physical rhythm.

Kalyanji Anandji made music but also were the shadow directors of the film *Don* made in 1978, and directed by Chandra Barot. Music directors often take to directing cinema, Hemant Kumar and Kishore Kumar being the best known among them. Cinematic images are moving images and what better way for them to move than through music? Indian popular cinematic images are designed and planned to produce music; music in cinema is more than being a mere accompaniment of the movement of narrative. Music is the outcome of the stories and the goal of our cinema.

Kalyanji Anandji were active in the Hindi film industry from 1960 to about 1994, and directed music for Shammi Kapoor, Rajendra Kumar and Dev Anand, but it was in Amitabh Bachchan that they seemed to have found their intrinsic essence. Kalyanji often would say in his interviews that Amitabh Bachchan is basically a singer and they made him sing in *Lawaaris*, and on live stage shows, made him sing Kishore Kumar numbers as well. Amitabh is a fairly prolific singer compared to other stars in the film industry; he has a natural understanding of beats and notes and this is why perhaps even though never been trained in either music or dance, he has also been able to start the trend of the dancing star.

Splits in the Image of Amitabh Bachchan

The Double Roles

One of the possible reasons for the vitality of the image of Amitabh Bachchan, its sustained appeal for the viewers and the repeated use of his histrionics in films, is perhaps due to the fact that his is an image with splits at several levels. There is a character split, a good man and a bad man as the film *Don* brings about. We see a similar split in the hero in *Satte Pe Satta* as well as in *Adalat, Kasme Vaade, Desh Premee, Mahaan* and few others. In these latter mentioned films, Amitabh has merely played a double role, with a triple role in *Mahaan*, the three roles being the jamboree of all the roles he has ever played across his films, but in *Don*, the good man tries to constantly impersonate the bad man, and in *Satte Pe Satta*, the opposite happens. The two roles enter into a dynamic with each other, one being absent and the one which is apparent, constantly strives to move towards the absence. What is more interesting is the realisation that Amitabh's unseen image becomes the focal point of the drama, making the hero more present when absent. The present image chases the absent one and hence moves beyond the contours of his existence in order to evolve into another kind of being. The hero moves between two sets of images, one of the dead Don and the other towards the naïve Vijay, and while Vijay is very much present and real, Don is dead, absent and has become past. The hero constantly covers the ground between the two images; one which is dead and retreating in memory and the other who is losing his innocence in order to look like the devilish Don.[1]

A major exception to the above trend is perhaps *Aakhri Raasta* and *Desh Premee*, in which the younger man and the older man, both played by Amitabh, argue against each other. The older man always wins and he dies as well; his death completes his existence and like in *Deewar*, vindicates his arguments.

The Origin of thc Doublc Rolc

The idea of the double role perhaps emerged from the writer Satish Bhatnagar of the film *Hera Pheri* in 1976, directed by Prakash Mehra. It is entirely possible that Prakash Mehra, while directing the angry young man in *Zanjeer*, may have thought that the film would be an instance of 'parallel' cinema and that he needed to return both Amitabh and himself to the mainstream cinema of the more 'normal' heroes. Amitabh in *Hera Pheri* was placed with a male co-star, namely Vinod Khanna.

This placing of Amitabh with a male co-star was to bring out more shades into the hero's character through constant competition, conflict and also great camaraderie. In the double roles, it is this male co-star who also gets played by Amitabh.

The hero was both, tragic as well as comic, contemplative as well as spontaneous and only a male co-star could bring about this duality as well as its integration. The formula of *Hera Pheri* led Salim Javed to write *Imaan Dharam* and Manmohan Desai completely created a whole new image with Amitabh as Anthony Gonsalves in *Amar Akbar Anthony* and thereafter.

---

1 Martin Heidegger. Being and Time. Harper Perennial. 1962. UK. 7th Edition. NY.2006. Pp 67-76

Salim Javed's Exiled Hero

There is a second level of split which is the one that Salim Javed created. This split is between a life which the hero was made out for and the life into which he is exiled. In *Zanjeer*, he could have been a happy child with his parents but he was orphaned, in *Deewar*, he could have lived a life of dignity and respectability but he was thrown into a life of poverty from which he could only return through the wrong route. Similarly, in *Trishul*, the character is abandoned by his biological father. In *Kala Patthar*, the hero exiles himself.

Salim Javed's split gives rise to the tragic hero; tragic because the exiled hero looks for reconciliation with his lost self, only to discover that that cannot be. The separation and yet the desire for reunion makes the hero pine for a world which he thought was merely lost only to realise that that which is lost cannot be found again. The split which leads to tragedy creates the core of the emotional appeal of the hero; the viewer feels a sense of loss within her, oscillating between longing and loss.

Mukul Anand's Separation of the Past and the Present

There is a third kind of a split which is the invention of Mukul Anand; this split is between the past and the present. The hero's valiant past is now only a memory and the world that needed his heroism is now changed, making him irrelevant. The present becomes useless to hold his talents, for the world which used to be his ground is now all gone. The present becomes empty, for there is neither the sense of longing nor loss for the past. Yet Mukul Anand's films bear intense tragedy and that tragedy emanates from the present being unable to relate to the past in any manner. In *Agneepath* and *Hum*, no one understands the capabilities of the hero, treats him as if he did not matter, takes him for granted without ever respecting that he made contributions, he suffered for others to be what they are at present. These films make the viewer seek the hero's death, for only in his absence can he be valued. Mukul Anand's films are tragic in a classic sense, for they leave no desire for reconciliation; happy endings seem anomalous.

Ram Gopal Varma's Split of the Body and the Mind

An important split in Amitabh's image is Ram Gopal Varma's essay of his role in *Sarkar*. The director takes the action image of Amitabh Bachchan and splits it into two in which he identifies a body that is activated in changing the situation and there is a mind that conceptualises that change and then deploys the body into action. The mind is held above the body, the bodily acts are then just seen as outcomes of a mind that ideates, plans and then deploys. This is why, Ram Gopal Varma could use Amitabh in his advancing years, showing him as a man immobile and even slightly disabled but an action hero nonetheless. Amitabh in *Sarkar* is an out an out action hero, but the physical aspect of the action is outsourced to his hired goons, while he himself conceptualises the action entirely in his head. *Sarkar's* portrayal of the action hero inspired Farhan Akhtar's *Wazir* and Sujoy Ghosh's *Te3n*.

The Advantage of the Split Image

The split image was crucial in creating a megastar out of Amitabh Bachchan because of the internal tension it created within the image. Tension is drama and Amitabh Bachchan became the locus of the drama all by himself and unto within himself. The rest of the film material with its characters and sub plots was absorbed into the persona of the hero in the film.

Tragedy

Two kinds of Tragedies[1]

Amitabh's image is founded upon tragedy and this is because of the split in his image. Even when he plays comic roles with gay abandon, the potential of tragedy does not disappear; for, tragedy is not only sorrow or pathos, but the impossibility of and yet the desire for reconciliation between moments and situations. The hero raises his standards very high, constructs himself in the Image of God, law, the protector, and the nourisher, all rolled into one, and yet fails to actualise himself in any of these roles. His self-image then is the image of the Divine, constrained by his being merely a mortal. This is the Hegelian notion of tragedy, idealistic and utopic mimicry of art, despite the lie of life. This is the tragedy of *Deewar*, of *Desh Premee*, and of *Aakhri Raasta*, in which the hero wants to bring about a perfect world for everyone, fails miserably, and dies in the end.

The other kind of tragedy which inheres Amitabh's image is a self that lies perpetually hidden, unexpressed, repressed and then lost forever. This self which is lost was due to him, belonged

1 Rowen Williams proposes two kinds of tragedies, one which is cosmic and adversely affects the individual while the other lies hidden, and is an inner split in persona that brings about a conflict of value within oneself. Rowen Williams. The Tragic Imagination. Oxford. UK. 2016. Pg 42 and pp 45-47.

rightfully to him and was one in which he could have had a much better life. But the hero loses his dues, derails in his path, and is exiled without the possibility of return. *Deewar*, *Zanjeer*, *Trishul* and even Manmohan Desai's films depict the hero's life in exile; he is separated from his family, a peaceful life which could be his, the respectability which he was born into but lost due to violence of humans or of unseen forces of fate. This separation creates a desire for reunion with the lost life; tragic because the reunion never quite takes place.

Tragedy creates Drama

Tragedy is the foundation of the dramatic in Amitabh Bachchan starrers. The lost life on the one hand and the idealist self on the other places a tension on the world of the present. On the one hand, he is cast into a life that is not due to him and hence he loses his selfhood. The loss of his self makes him into his own alter ego. The hero does not resent his marginalisation; instead, he works within its logic, which produces a self that threatens that very same order that had exiled him. The logic of the exile creates an antihero out of him, without those values which can uphold the status quo but with those values which challenge the system. The logic of his existence that makes the status quo feels threatened, reveals that the system does not want the hero to live. The hero faces the death wish of the establishment and indeed does face death in many of his movies. The hero and the world cannot coexist, and this creates a constant tussle in the narrative. The villain is actually incidental, more of a prop to create opportunities for us to witness the hero's bodily actions. The real drama of Amitabh Bachchan starrers are the arguments of the hero against the order.

Tragedy is Political

Amitabh's films are intensely political because of the logic of arguments. The hero is thrown into abject poverty in most of Amitabh's films. The world of poverty has its own ways of working and when the hero tries to work through the poverty trap and emerge into respectability, he discovers that his perfectly logical activities are construed as being illegitimate by law. The hero proves that the law aims to protect only the status quo, with its system of exclusive entitlements and its property relations. There is a world which is devoid of such means of livelihood and should that world try to attain similar material goods of the entitled world, law is unleashed as violence to exterminate the claimants. The violence of law that separates the classes and defends the separation as sacred makes tragedy of the films of Amitabh Bachchan political.

Tragedy Makes a Super Star

Tragedy made a superstar out of Amitabh Bachchan. One is more used to Dilip Kumar being called the tragic star of Hindi films, and the epithet of tragedy might seem a bit facetious for Amitabh Bachchan to bear. Dilip Kumar's tragedy is personal; it inheres within him as an emotion. Amitabh's tragedy is the inner paradox of systems, of universes, of cognitive labyrinths, of personal histories. Since the hero's tragedy concerns not his individual self but the world he inhabits, through tragedy, the hero becomes the world. His superstardom is the symptom of the personal graduating into the ethical.

Anger and Violence

Anger and Violence are not Linked in the Image

Anger and violence appear to be the two manifestations of the image of Amitabh Bachchan, known as the Angry Young Man of Hindi films. It appears as if the hero is angry, and in that anger, he becomes violent. But looked at carefully, anger and violence are two distinct moments of the image. Anger is really directed at no specific individual; it is resentment, like in *Deewar,* saying that please go and get them to sign on the papers who ruined my father, who molested my mother, who insulted and humiliated me because I am what I am because of these people; this anger is general and not directed at any one in particular. In *Zanjeer*, he is just angry because he is has lost his memory. In *Trishul*, he is angry with his father but not violent towards him. In *Kala Paththar*, the hero is angry with himself but not violent, and similarly, in *Kabhie Kabhie*, a veneer of anger surrounds the hero but he is not violent. Indeed, in the grand fight in the warehouse with Peter and his gang in *Deewar,* there was violence, but anger was overcome, only to later emerge again in one of the most solitary and silent moments.

Interestingly, Yash Chopra raised anger to the hero's overall consciousness, so that Amitabh also looked romantic in addition to angryin *Kabhie Kabhie*. In films like *Kaalia*, *Satte Pe Satta*, and even in *Naseeb*, *Namakhalal* and others, he shows the capability of putting up a great fight without being angry in a sustained manner.

Violence for Amitabh as a hero is the execution of a sentence; often sterile of anger that pronounced the sentence in the first place. The separation of anger from violence has been able to turn Amitabh's image into that of an appellant, a judge and the executioner, all into one. Anger that wells up inside the hero and which he sublimates into a discourse of justice, transforms him from merely being a victim of fate into a revolutionary who thinks of a new world. These are the moments of emerging from victimhood into a thinker that the appellant turns into the judge. In moments of violence, the hero is perhaps more peaceful and the penultimate scenes of *Sholay*, *Trishul*, *Kala Paththar*, *Aakhri Raasta*, *Andha Kanoon* are very good examples of this.

However, in the later films, especially those of Manmohan Desai like *Coolie*, *Mard*, *Toofan* and in K.C.Bokadia's *Aaj Ka Arjun*, violence became both personal and political, because clear villains were identified, who were personifications of an entire regime. The hero in Amitabh Bachchan represents not merely a person, but an entire order of thought, a set of principles, an ethical system and now, in the later films, the villains also came to represent entire systems and thoughts. Corresponding to a superstar hero, the villain also had to be a superstar. At the level of the image and especially the body movements, this posed a danger of the hero and the villain drawing close to each other. Vigorous violence separated the two.

Violence as a Capability[1]

Violence was a capability of the hero to defend him and to protect his loved ones against the random violence of the public sphere. The middle class, the repertoire of the value system in India, however was unable to defend itself in the face of violence from the society at large; its travel was marred by violence in the roads,

1 Frantz Fanon. The Wretched of the Earth. Penguin. London. Reprinted 200. Pg 73.

its free movement obstructed by the fear of being physically hurt, and it lived under the threat of bodily harm from the goons. Amitabh reversed all of this, for he could fight to defend himself and therefore everything else that he stood for, his ideology, his values and his morals.

Action Image

Deleuze in his classification of the images in cinema said that the essence of cinema was the movement image. The movement image was not the moving image in which an image would merely move but images in cinema are about movement, not merely a change in space covered but 'an act of covering'[1]. Deleuze derives their theories from the idea of consciousness of Henri Bergson, in which Bergson says that consciousness is produced by sensing physically aspects of the external stimuli. Hence, movement produces a consciousness which is closely related to the exercise of agency of the individual; individual agency whereby the individual creates the conditions of her own existence is modernity and no other form of art other than cinema can represent modernity as well.[2]

Movement is not space covered, it is the act of covering and which is why the theorists say that cinema is inherently incomplete, for movement can happen only when the whole is not given. In cinema, it is not only one privileged image that is moving but every image is moving, which means that the movement is relative to many other kinds of movements, sometimes in opposition and at other times in convergence.

---

1 Gilles Deleuze. Cinema 1. Continuum. London. First South Asian Edition. 2005. pp 4-8.

2 Ibid pp 1-3

Accordingly, there are three kinds of movement images; namely the perception image, the affect image and the action image. The perception image remains more or less at the centre, absorbing movement from the other images, remaining as the point of view around which movement takes place. Such images are typical of Dilip Kumar and even Dev Anand. Javed Akhtar has commented many times on the way Dilip Kumar would observe women, making them emerge in their movements gloriously.[3] Dev Anand often played the sleuth, the CID and even the secret agent in which he was the observer.

The second kind of movement image is the affection image, the image which is the close up, the one who sees but is seen by the audience; the emotions that well up in this image is a temporary suspension of movement; an arrest in the act of covering space. Guru Dutt and Raj Kapoor seem to be instances of such kind of movement image.

The third kind of movement image is the action image, the image that can change the situation in its act of covering. The action image can further be divided into the broad frame and the small frame. The broad frame action image is the one in which the actor changes the situation from one kind to another kind; which is being changed is constraining and which is being changed to is redemptive. The narrow kind is the one in which the actor, out of her habit, acts on a situation, more out of her natural instinct or out of impulse to redeem herself rather than the situation.

The image of Amitabh Bachchan is an action image of both the broad and the narrow kinds. The action image is one that carries the situation and the actor reflects the situation, emerges from within it and her final image is a state of victory. Victory has been so attached to Amitabh's image that his screen name, Vijay, which means victory, has stuck onto him. It is only the action image that can be victorious; the rest of the images can survive, thrive, sustain and be gone through. Victory is a change in the

---

3 Javed Akhtar on Dilip Kumar. Jaane Pehchaane. Epic Channel. Season 2. Episode 4.

conditions of the non-victorious, a situational transformation, and a change in the conditions of existence, and hence, is a broad range of action. In the words of Martin Heidegger who combined the Hegelian idealism with a French existentialism, the action image is a series of constantly dissolving the various states of being. The action image of Amitabh constantly dissolves his boundaries in order to act upon the world with an intention of changing it. He does not merely 'make it out in the world'; instead, he wishes to change the very conditions of life so that he can access another level of existence from which flow rewards, which the hero's present condition cannot deliver. No wonder that rags to riches story belongs very securedly to Amitabh Bachchan. Mallika Sherawat spoke of Amitabh Bachchan's image as one of a runner, and I think that running is the basic flavour of Amitabh's action image, running to cover the ground from poverty to prosperity, from being marginalised into being reckoned into the mainstream, from being a victim into becoming a victor.

Images of the above mentioned filmstars are a combination of the various categories of images classified by Deleuze. Dilip Kumar was both a perception as well as an affection image; Dev Anand was a perception and a narrow-range action hero. Sunil Dutt is affection and narrow-range action, Shatrughan Sinha, a narrow-range action and an affection image. Dharmendra, who like Amitabh, also has a split image, is perception and affection in one and perception and narrow-range action in another. No star so far in the Hindi popular cinema has been a broad-range action image nearly in a pure form as Amitabh Bachchan has been. Raj Kapoor must have been a master of images, for he combined the perception, the affection and the broad-range action image, all in a single imagery. Raj Kapoor, like Amitabh Bachchan, is intensely political; he works, like the broad-range action hero, against opposition, but he maintains the personal and the political distinctly apart. Amitabh's politics subsumes the personal, his childhood, his affections and sometimes his love life, but no star has such purely a broad frame action image, perception, affection and even the narrow range actions all emanating out of the broad range action image.

In Manmohan Desai's films, Amitabh becomes a narrow-range action image in which he fights to express his brawn, more as an instinct, because he has been challenged by individuals rather than by the situation. The montage of Manmohan Desai's films are full of people, totally privileging the multi-starrers. Amitabh becomes local not situational, he is born as someone and remains as that someone, adapting and accepting gracefully his situation rather than transcending it as in as in *Zanjeer* or *Deewar*, or *Trishul* or *Kala Paththar*.

The action image of Amitabh Bachchan breaks the mould of the Hindi film hero who operated within the precincts of a middle-class world; action made the hero emerge out of his entrenchment into his specific social class and become a universal person. The hero of the conventional Hindi mainstream cinema, remains even today a person who tries to be the ideal; Amitabh tries to be victorious. Amitabh carries within his persona not much of ideals as much as ideology; his image is one of class conflict, hugely useful in politics of social competition in democracies championing equality.

Death and Dying

Death and dying have been important for the image of Amitabh Bachchan. Of some 200 odd films, Amitabh Bachchan has died in about a tenth of them, but the motif of death remains rather central to his star persona. Strangely, death is not tragic for Amitabh because it does not truncate him or demolish him; death braces his life, completes his mission, and vindicates his beliefs; death for Amitabh is a glorious consummation to his struggles. This is perhaps because Amitabh's image is a series of dissolutions, of evolution, of emergence into higher states of existence; death brings the process to fruition.

There are stars who died onscreen: Rajesh Khanna dies in *Anand* and *Safar*, Dilip Kumar in *Ganga Jumna*, Sunil Dutt in *Mother India*, Rajendra Kumar in *Dil Ek Mandir* and Raj Kapoor in *Mera Naam Joker*, and these are among the most mentionable deaths onscreen. But there are differences among the deaths; not all are of the same kind. Rajesh Khanna's death is untimely and he dies leaving an enormous vacuum. We desire he return to us as in *Aradhana*, and in *Anand* we cling to the taped words, preserving him forever with us. Indeed, Rajesh Khanna's stardom seemed to have been resurrected with his real life demise; with his funeral, he seems to have got his superstardom back after having lived nearly four decades of invisibility, away from public reckoning.

Dilip Kumar's death in *Ganga Jumna* is tragic, being shot down by his own brother, who despite himself, had to prevent the star from abrogating the law. This death was a greater tragedy for the killer, the younger brother who despite his love for the older sibling, had to pull the trigger. It was similar to Sunil Dutt's death in *Mother India*, where Nargis, in her role as a mother, had to gun her favourite son down as a disciplining act. The tragedy of death once again was upon the killer and not one who was dead. Rajendra Kumar died like a martyr in *Dil Ek Mandir*, dead from sheer exhaustion in trying to save his lover's husband's life in the operation theatre. Death emerged for the hero played by Rajendra Kumar as a face-saving grace, for his fiancée being married to another man and being still in love with him would have been extremely embarrassing. Death is an exit, a face saver.

Amitabh's death in *Deewar* and *Agneepath* seems to be a logical extension of the body, a body that has carried too much action for the world to bear; it had been an equilibrium-upsetting action, an action that created too big a scope for liberation than what the world could hold, and hence, the hero died out of the earth's inability to accommodate him. Amitabh's death on screen established the hero as being too big for the world to have him anymore; instead of the hero dying an exhausted death, it is the world which gets exhausted with the hero's life, so his death brings back the equilibrium. The hero's death is a tragedy for us, a lost opportunity for the society he lived in, the community among who he worked. Death establishes the hero in his larger than life image in cinema. Death makes the hero mortal, so he remains with the world and does not transcend it. Death is the only way to contain and hence, regard the largeness of the hero. In death, the hero's life gets a frame around it, without which it would have been impossible for him to be contained. Death completes *Deewar's* hero, makes him into a tightly woven text, leaving no scope for improvisation. No wonder it has been impossible to make *Deewar* again.

In *Piku*, a film released in 2015, in which Amitabh acted as the nit picking, ageing widower and a father to an only unmarried and working daughter, death comes as a fruition of a life well lived. This death is therefore inconsequential, a natural step forward for the image the character lived in. Amitabh's death in *Desh Premee*, in *Adalat* and even in *Aakhri Raasta* have been similarly inconsequential, leaving no one sad really. But it was in *Muqaddar Ka Sikandar* that the hero dies; dies somewhat in defiance of the Heavens, dies in defiance to his destiny. For it was here he could have lived on but he decided not to, choosing death as an exit to leave his love interest undisturbed with hers. Death for the hero of *Muqaddar Ka Sikandar* is an exercise of his power and also of his love; his ultimate erotic energies unable to find expression upon earth are redeemed in death. Few deaths in Bollywood cinema can be said to have this kind of sex appeal as the one of Amitabh Bachchan in *Muqaddar Ka Sikandar*.

There are however two instances in which the death of the hero left a sense of yearning for him and these two are *Sholay* and *Don*. Indeed, when Farhan Akhtar remade *Don*, he did not let Don die and instead made Vijay, the impersonator be exterminated. In the original version, Don dies and Vijay, a simpleton, is made to step into the role of the dreaded Don. Amitabh Bachchan plays both the roles; as Vijay, he constantly tries to reach Don, the background score by Kalyanji Anandji establishes through the tempo of the beat this continuous chase of Don by his detractors as well as Vijay's chase to reach the level of Don's suaveness, stealth and skills. Don is deadly but we miss Don because it was his deadliness that was the centre of the story; the story was to emerge out of Don, the narrative was to be controlled by the character, manipulated and twisted in all manners by his lethal attributes. Vijay is played by Amitabh Bachchan but more as a performance, bereft of the character of star persona. As Vijay undergoes his training to emerge as Don, we see the non-persona rising to meet the persona of the dreaded smuggler. The rhythm rises too in a staccato as does Vijay in his attempts at catching up with the great Don.

The death of the star in *Sholay* was intended to create a vacuum in the story, leave a gaping hole in it by which the vendetta and violence would all sink into leaving us with peace. *Sholay* is about war but also the end of it, about the inevitability of war and yet its futility. Jai's death, the character played by Amitabh, seemed to end the circle of violence suddenly, stunning us into a silence and then releasing us into an emptiness, turning that vendetta tale into a void. *Sholay* was indeed Amjad's film but because Jai dies, Amitabh lends a strange immortality to *Sholay* on the whole and in that sense, also claims and even partially appropriates it.

We may bring Martin Heidegger once more here when he says that for the being who seems to evolve continuously, never reaching the totality of her being, always in search for something, death brings the finality.[1]

1 Martin Heidegger. Being and Time. Harper and Row. New York. 1962. Republished Harperperennial. New York. 208. Pp 288-289. Para 244-245.

Divinity and Punishment

No male star is as well known for his relationship with God as Amitabh Bachchan. In *Deewar* he is God's sworn enemy and challenges God while praying to Him and in *Amar Akbar Anthony*, the hero considers God as his buddy, for he feels blessed. The idea of Divine is interestingly developed through the image of Amitabh Bachchan across his films.

The hero is a person who thinks holistically; he places the source of his trouble in the legal and ethical framework of the State, he argues with law and jurisprudence, he looks far into the genesis of causes and identifies the root cause of troubles into the troubles of his childhood. It is as if that he can connect like a spider's web all points of his life and integrate his experiences into envisioning a logical whole. This holism in his approach is his Divinity. The idea and ideation of an order, a holistic and a systematic Universe is the hero's Divinity.

Once the hero has made a logical connection of the entirety of his existence and his interaction with the world, a web of interconnectedness will lie before him. This makes him capable of anticipation, forecast and the agility to do things strategically, and he can also understand far better his own role in shaping the world as also his limitations. The mosaic of interconnections that open up before him, revealing his role in the shape of things which have been and those which possibly can be due to his interventions makes him wholly in command of his own life. In *Adalat* and *Aakhri Raasta*, films made a decade apart from each other, even in a hilarious film like *Namakhalal* or in *Lawaaris*, the hero knows everything that goes on behind his back, identifies the miscreants and eliminates or traps them. The enlarged and expanded consciousness of the hero is his divinity.

Were Hegel to live to see Amitabh Bachchan, he would have commented that Amitabh's divinity comes from the hero's mistaken assumption that life is art, aesthetics being the perfect unity of opposite forces engaged in dialectics and resolving the oppositions by transcending into a higher level of reality. Amitabh's tragedy is the naivety to believe that life can be an art and hence, he neither remains happy with art nor is satisfied with life.

In contrast to the above, the hero in Manmohan Desai's *Amar Akbar Anthony, Naseeb*, or *Desh Premee*, the hero is unaware of the quirks of fates and the conspiracies that surround him. The hero is surrendered to the processes at work and free of them because he is so wholly and entirely immersed in them that he loses all awareness of being consumed by his situation. His complete surrender to his situation in Manmohan Desai's films is his divinity.

It is perhaps due to Amitabh's imagination of the Divine as being his own essence that Amitabh often becomes punitive. In *Kala Paththar,* he exiles himself, in *Mahaan* he literally whips himself till he bleeds profusely, in *Kabhie Kabhie* and *Silsila* he disciplines himself and in *Muqaddar Ka Sikandar,* he sacrifices himself at the altar of the Divine. He is sensitive to order, and any slight deviation irritates him since life for him is art, intolerant of imperfections. This intolerance makes him punishing; he thrashes the miscreants as mercilessly as he flagellates himself. The idea that life must be perfect, makes Amitabh into some kind of a rigid and a self-absorbed person who is disturbed by imperfections and punishes them to restore order. No wonder then the roles of policemen suit the star so well and when he stands against law, punishing the law maker and the judge, he shakes the establishment in its foundations.

Amitabh in Manmohan Desai's film is not a punishing person; in fact, in these films, he abandons the language of rights, has no arguments around law, does not purport to be the judge, and does not invoke higher principles or heavy morals. He is spontaneous; can and will fight villains when required. Only in much later films like *Mard*, the hero played by Amitabh develops a self-righteousness and vigilantist and moral anger, perhaps in competition with the images of the hero created by Prakash Mehra. Manmohan Desai's films project Amitabh Bachchan as a man integrated with the community and not aloof from his world, staying away from things with a critique, or wallowing in regret about why life must not be orderly as he desires it to be.

Silence and Fury

Amitabh is vocal and voluble and is famous for ear-hammering dialogues in berating tones, reprimanding and disapproving the police, the judge, the politician and of course the capitalist, his villains being one or more of the above. Amitabh's baritone, his diction, his pauses, command over language, and the modulation of delivery have enriched our film-viewing experience. Indeed, Amitabh Bachchan received a fan letter written in Braille! This must be among his prized possessions. Notwithstanding the voice and the volume of the star, there is also a deep silence contained in the image. The hero is silent in his meditations in *Zanjeer* and *Adalat*, he is solitary in *Sholay* when he sits all by himself in the night playing the mouth organ, he is silent in *Mahaan* when he quietly and secretly self flagellates himself and he is silent when he conspires to kill his wife's murderers in *Aakhri Raasta*. These are moments when the hero is silent. Journalists, co-stars, directors, peers and friends are constantly curious about what Amitabh Bachchan has to say, hanging on to anything he may utter, eager to hear more of him and this is despite the fact that Amitabh is verbose in his blog, tweets regularly and posts his political opinions, and is surprisingly open to the press. Yet, we think that Amitabh is more silent than uttered.

The silence of Amitabh, according to my understanding, has two distinct sources. Amitabh gets the same set of directors, scriptwriters, choreographers and music directors to work with, and yet, it is strange the way in which he turns and twists everything to emerge as a superstar. Behind the dialogues he delivers, dance moves he makes, close ups and various other emotions he may express, there is still an unsolved mystery as to how he can do everything better than the rest. This large hidden area from which Amitabh Bachchan fires the salvos remains totally inaccessible by inquisitive observers and unspoken by the star. This cloud cover is the source of silence. No wonder when he recites in Silsila, *'main aur meri tanhaiy aksar yeh batein karte hain'*, it becomes an articulation of the silence in the hero essayed by Amitabh, in which reticence is reflective dialogue.

The other source of silence lies within the film; just as Amitabh's action emanated from a system of thought behind it and which made him into an action hero even in films like *Sarkar* and *Vazir* where he barely could move because action came from his mind though someone else did the physical activity for him; similarly the loquacious dialogues were also generated from a deep zone of silence in which much meditation and reflection had gone into the understanding of the situation. As mentioned in an earlier essay that Amitabh's action is broad-based in the sense that the hero acts upon the situation in order to change it; he does not merely respond to the situation. This is why his actions and dialogues which are verbal counterparts of his physical actions also emerge from long reflections, instead of being reactions to the external stimuli. The unspoken reflection that gives rise to dialogues constitutes the huge silence behind the spoken word.

Age

Stars have an innate age like the quizzes that keep appearing on gaming sites like what is your real age? Jaya Bhaduri is Guddi at heart, a teenager who never quite grows up, Nirupa Roy has never been young. Shammi is a young man in his early twenties while Raj Kapoor and others are in their late twenties. Amitabh Bachchan is a man of matured years, a man who is at that age at which he has seen done all. There is not only a maturity and insight of years, but his is a face of having absorbed life in no small measure, a holism in thought that is not possible without a distance which the passions of youth cannot attain. He is a man who may have longed and lost, but we have no data about his youthful follies. He is a man beyond mistakes, a man who never relents to his desires, lives for his family and the world at large, a survivor and a fighter who battles to protect his ilk rather than to glorify himself in victory. He is indifferent to his own condition, rarely ever raises a hand for himself, but if it is to save a helpless young person, educate brothers, raise orphans, rescue sister and to make mother comfortable, the hero leaves no stone unturned. This indifference towards one's desires and the transcendence of passions, gives the star a heaviness of age.

In films in which Amitabh is cast in a double role, a younger man and an older man, it has always been the older man who is the protagonist of the film. Films like *Adalat*, *Aakhri Raasta*,

Desh Premee and *Suryavansham* are points in the case. The innate maturity of years in Amitabh has perhaps sustained him in his biological old age when he continues to be as attractive to his fans as he was about four decades ago.

The Political Image

In today's times when politics and cinema has come close to each other and politics has assumed the stature of popular culture, one may not be surprised with film stars joining politics. Both Prithviraj Kapoor and Nargis have been members of the Rajya Sabha, but it was Amitabh who also led the trend of film stars contesting political elections and winning to enter the lower house of the Parliament. Amitabh Bachchan had been close to the family of Mrs Indira Gandhi, and indeed Rajeev and Sonia stayed with the Bachchans before they were married, so when Mrs Gandhi was assassinated and Rajiv Gandhi was slated to become the Prime Minister, he called his friends to his side in order to tide over a duty he was not experienced in. Amitabh Bachchan was among his friends who joined politics at the calling of Rajiv Gandhi. Amitabh eventually resigned on graft charges, those which were later disproved and his name was cleared beyond doubt, but the bitterness of the brief stint at politics was enough to make the star say that he would not like to touch politics with a barge pole. Amitabh admitted that he understood nothing of politics and that the trade was a veritable 'cesspool'. Later, he did seek political patronage from a variety of non-Congress parties, changed loyalties frequently among them and seems to have emerged more as an opportunist than one who is apolitical.[1]

The real life and reel life thus are clearly apart for Amitabh Bachchan because in cinema, his image is political. It is political because Amitabh as the hero is more concerned about villains, the law and the State that impinges upon his work life. He seems to be more concerned with his productive powers rather than the reproductive powers, like the girl he wants to marry. As early as in *Kabhie Kabhie*, Amitabh gives up his inspiration in the form of the girl he loved and diverted his focus to his work. Romances come only as an appendage, more to keep to the routine of the Hindi film formula. Amitabh's productive and not his biological reproduction was the focus of the films. The popular cinema used to be mainly a matter of the family versus the individual, but in Amitabh's films, the family as a whole is under siege from the violence of the society, the individual becomes unhinged from the family and is depersonalised in a mean, scurrilous, demeaning public space. This makes law and governance into a major issue in the lives of individuals in Amitabh starrers and hence, his films are political. The image of the hero is political because he engages with the State.

However, in films like *Trishul* and *Kala Paththar*, and especially so in Manmohan Desai's films where despite the police and the law, the hero has no direct conflict with the State, films retain their political flavour because the hero is wrenched out of his moorings in the family, extracted from a family life and is atomised and alienated in the world without any institution of the society to contain him. In *Amar Akbar Anthony*, the three characters by these names are brothers and they have parents as well, but each is separated from the other, one not knowing the whereabouts of the others. Such an unchaperoned world makes a person encounter the public space which only the State can order.

---

1 http://www.openthemagazine.com/article/art-culture/kabhi-here-kabhi-there, "A Man of No Convictions"

The hero in an Amitabh starrer is usually born poor and helpless and he overcomes his fate; so had Rajesh Khanna in *Haathi Mere Saathi*, or Shatrughan Sinha in *Vishwanath*. But in the Amitabh starrers, the hero raises his struggles not to the level of individual exertions but into the discourse of a class struggle. As a hero, Amitabh recalls that his initial displacement was a power struggle in the society, a society that uses its legal system, its police and the institutions of the state to maintain the asymmetry of power and inequalities in property relations, so that the social opportunities forever reach unequally and maintains the inequalities inherent in the society. This makes Amitabh Bachchan the star into a political image.

Masculinity versus Femininity

It is said that Amitabh Bachchan was a tectonic shift in Hindi popular cinema because he reoriented the concerns of cinema with those of the purity and integrity of its women, with a concern for making way for the upward social mobility of the male. Amitabh's films were concerned with work, productive powers, relations of equality in property and in equal social opportunities, irrespective of the inequalities in social entitlements one was born with. The hero strove for meritocracy and was the talented man of Koditscheck, the inventor, the scientist, essentially a bachelor[1]. Indeed, such a person in every society across humanity is usually imagined to be a male, even though the achiever in question is a woman scientist or an astronaut or a detective. Amitabh flavours the cinema with masculinity, with his male bachelorhood. No wonder then gossips and speculations never cease about Amitabh Bachchan's possible sexual exploits and his continued liaison with Rekha, his co-star and supposed love interest.

Carl Jung says in his work, *The Aspects of the Masculine,* that masculinity is of many types; at one level it is growing up and

---

1 Theodore Koditschek. "Genius and the Household Model Of Intellectual Production. (1795 – 1885)" in Journal of Social History. Volume 39. No 2. Winter 2005. Pp 429-449.

realising one's sexuality.[2] The Hindi film heroes are usually ones who are realising their sexuality by being attracted to women and contemplating sexual unions. Amitabh's existence is threatened in his films and so he needs to emerge into a level of an entrepreneur, a man of knowledge and a man of self-commanding authority, so that he can change the conditions of his existence. In this, he becomes the wise man, the father, and even the Divine by taking full charge of his life and also commanding the material conditions, should they rise to threaten his existence. Amitabh's masculinity, in terms of Jung's work, is thus, one of authority, command, knowledge and extreme rationality beyond sexual tensions. He is masculine precisely because he has really no need for the feminine.

Yet, interestingly, Amitabh's image could have well been that of a woman. Carl Jung says that when the masculine is defined as being an authority of man unto himself, it may inhere in women as well. Jung mentions that the Almighty female is similar to the Almighty male and both are actually beyond gender or are gender neutral.

Amitabh's image of the talented bachelor, the lone scientist, is useful in the politics of his image, for in an industrial society, especially the times in which he lived, the male was the source of upward social mobility; upward social mobility in which the asset class changes, if not the property relations (who owns more money and entitlements and who doesn't), is political and because this involves the engagement of the individuals with the outside world, something which represents the masculine, the hero's image is masculine. The hero constantly struggles against other men, against force, using force, extending his physical body, all of which are metaphors of male sexuality. Amitabh uses his inner resources and inner strength to engage and overcome the world; this struggle from the inside to the outside perhaps resembles the male sexual act. In other heroes,

---

2. Carl Jung. Aspects of the Masculine. Routledge Special Indian Edition. London. 2003. Pg 18. Para 456.

the enjoyment of the world by absorbing the pleasures into the body might well then be the extension of the female sexuality into the male body.

In the image of masculinity that could transcend the feminine, Amitabh's image as a hero seceded the need to have a feminine counterpart. This rendered the woman quite 'useless' as a companion for the soul and reduced her to a need based fulfilment of baser instincts. No wonder the image of the heroine became that of a mere body without any finer qualities that would grace the heroines before Amitabh Bachchan's days. Parveen Babi, Zeenat Aman and even Rekha were there to sexually allure the hero, otherwise indifferent to sex. Rekha and Zeenat Aman acted in many films without Amitabh and they did far better in those productions.

Yet, at another level, the image of Amitabh absorbed the feminine by becoming the nourisher and the protector of the family. The hero has no purpose of his own except to protect his family and of those who are helpless and need his care. The image of the hero as a protector and a nourisher absorbed the feminine by appropriating the feminine into him. It is interesting that much excitement also ensued in films over the Nirupa Roy and Amitabh Bachchan pair, in which they played mother and son.

A Life Without a Father

I think that a major difference between Rajesh Khanna and Amitabh Bachchan has been the images they held of themselves as children. Rajesh Khanna, born and lived as Jatin Khanna, was raised by his father's older brother and his wife as their own son. His life was similar to Prince Gautama, except that Rajesh Khanna went onto become the king rather than the ascetic Buddha. In his childhood, says Yasser Usman, in his biography of Bollywood's first superstar, Jatin lived as if he was a prince and which he was, given the fact that he was raised in luxury. Amitabh Bachchan, on the other hand, was raised in a middle-class family setup that was constituted out of the intelligentsia. Living in a university campus, ensconced among scholarly and litterateur colleagues of his father, a poet of eminence, Harivansh Rai Bachchan, Amitabh was raised to be a modern man, an ideal citizen of India, which in those days would mean well educated, cultured and a sensible mix of modernity and tradition. The difference in the upbringing clearly explains the differences in the persona of the two superstars who crossed each other in film space and in time.

Harivansh Rai Bachchan had left home to be away at Cambridge pursuing his doctorate degree when Amitabh, at the age of 10, became the head of the family. Amitabh speaks to

Soumya Bandopadhyay[1] in a tone in which Babur writes in his autobiography that he at the age of 13 became the king of Ferghana when his father, Mirza Baig died by falling into the gorge after the dovecot collapsed. Teji Bachchan, nee Suri, Amitabh's mother, was a capable and a highly-educated woman, and it is difficult to believe that she would need a 10-year-old son to be the head of the household and so this must have been a way to make Amitabh have something to do while his father was away so that he would miss him less. Nonetheless, the play act of being a father when his father was absent was indelibly marked into the Amitabh Bachchan star image. In *Deewar*, the hero takes upon himself the role of a protector of his mother and infant brother while he is still a child and much is the same in *Agneepath*. Through the narrative flow of the film, the image of the star takes upon himself the role of a decision maker, incorporating within the screen persona a mental resolve of strategising and making the montage move through the consciousness of the protagonist. He is a person of authority and with this, integrates film material into his consciousness; his authority creates a reason for the various montages to converge into a single point, often the conclusion of the story. Just as a father would rise to discipline his children to fall in line, the exercise of paternal authority of the characters played by Amitabh has a similar manner of disciplining and therefore, tightening the film script.

The authority of the father is spread to the containment of other images as well. Even when Amitabh acts in multi-starrers, he seems to dominate the screen as well; perhaps because of a personality brought up and chaperoned by parents who were more of his facilitators rather than disciplinarians. Amitabh recalls how his parents would reason with him, argue with him, hear his point of view and even support him in all his endeavours. Once, writes Soumya Bandopadhyay, in his boarding school, Amitabh was supposed to act in a play but he developed high fever.

---

1 Soumya Bandopadhyay. Amitabh Bachchan. Bengali. Ananda Publishers. Kolkata. 1995.

Deeply upset with this illness, he brooded in the sick room. His father then told him his famous lines, *jo manka ho, who achha hai, jo man ka nahi ho, who aur bhi achha hai*, meaning what is to your heart's desire is good but what is not to your heart's desire is even better. Father has been a mentor and not a figure who claimed authority over the son as a matter of right, and thus, raising Amitabh as a person of reasoned decisions rather than as a rebel without a cause. The so-called rebellion that was in the hero's heart was more of an extension of authority to create a fair world rather than the despair of a lost soul. The rebellion was the act of establishing one's own kingdom rather than to wage a war against the ruler.

In *Deewar*, the hero fights for the dead Nandu, a young man who dies a martyr to raising a protest against the goons of the dockyard and the hero is awakened to the memories of his father being wronged by a similar set of goons long ago. He fights for Nandu with a force which he believed could have saved his father's life, were someone to exert it. He tells Rahim Chacha, the elderly porter, who worries for the hero's safety, that he must fight Nandu's murder only because he wants to eliminate the violence of the miscreants; he wishes to eliminate violence at its source. The hero of *Deewar*, called Vijay, is at once the father when he disciplines the miscreants and saving Nandu (Nandu is already dead but he wants no one else like Nandu to die) and also a son who by 'saving' Nandu 'saves' his father, a trade union leader, from being lynched by an angry mob. In the montage in which Vijay fights the goons, one feels as though he is avenging his father's humiliation and indeed when the crowd carries him on their shoulders, we get a very similar pattern on screen of the father being carried by a crowd of admiring workers when he fights their case. The montage tells us that Vijay had become his father.

For the image of the hero, the act of becoming the father is both an organic growth of the film as well as its so-called pathetic interval. For indeed, the son has to grow up to be the father, but there is also the responsibility of becoming the father hurled at him by misfortune. Amitabh's image is thus slightly stooped with the burden of responsibilities; the face is a bit ruminative with the insight of age which is beyond his years. In films like *Adalat*, *Desh Premee* and *Aakhri Raasta*, in which Amitabh plays a double role of an older man and a younger one, it is always the older man who is the protagonist. Now that Amitabh is really old now in years, roles keep flowing to him because he has always kept within his persona, a maturity, which reflects the rare wisdom of experience.

Interestingly, in *Agneepath*, the hero, also called Vijay, has also stepped into the shoes of his dead father. Unlike in *Deewar*, in which the father is missing and emerges only as flashes across the scene in moving trains, the father in *Agneepath* is dead. Vijay knows this, and while keeps the memories of his father alive, trying to avenge his death, unlike in *Deewar*, there is no lurking hope to find his father again. In terms of cinematic image, this pans out in an interesting way; the figure of the hero is less restrained, more freewheeling and self-willed just as sons would be when their fathers are no longer around to be conscious of.

The essence of Amitabh's screen persona is the father and not the orphan which the hero becomes when father dies or disappears; none have played better orphans than Raj Kapoor and Mithun Chakravarty in their films. Central Asia takes these two film stars as part of their myth.

Comedy

No discussion on the image of Amitabh Bachchan is complete without a discussion of his comic image. It was not only the heroines who lost jobs in the film industry but the comedian as well became pretty much redundant after Amitabh overwhelmingly took over the comic roles. Manmohan Desai must be credited with the discovery of the comedian within Amitabh Bachchan. The effectiveness of Amitabh's comedy stems from the fact that his is an innately stern and a severe image with a tendency to punish and get even. Amitabh's is a feared image and when it becomes a bit undone as in a comic role, it becomes a very effective rendition.

Much like Amitabh's trade mark of one who fights the villains, his comedy also undoes the other. It is also a powerful tool of punishing others as well as of self-infliction of punitive sentences. In the famous mirror scene of *Amar Akbar Anthony*, the hero dresses the wounds of his own reflection in the mirror; in *Kasme Vaade* he negotiates with a cockroach and in *Namakhalal*, he slaps nasty people on the pretext of squashing a fly. Amitabh's comedy is not beyond his action frame; it is yet another way to position his basic image and perhaps, this is why his roles as a comedian have not been able to undo his essential image of an action hero, and in fact, seemed to have reinforced the same.

The Romantic Image – Union of Opposites

Frank Kermode's work on the romantic image as a set of essays on the Romantic Movement in literature says that the idea of romance is not a sexual union of the male and the female, but an inner integration of joy and sorrow, movement and stillness, voice and silence, and life and death. Kermode says that this is the image of the dancer in Yeats.[1] Amitabh's image is strangely similar to this idea of unity of opposites. We have discussed in an earlier essay that Amitabh had a split image, an image that would integrate seemingly opposite characteristics, of action and stillness, of revenge and letting go, of excessive application yet a resignation, of sternness and affection, of being a loner and yet a great attachment to family, of great speed in catching up and yet a patient waiting to wind up inner strength and resources, quick action and yet detailed planning. The unity of opposites provides the hero with self-fulfillment and an autonomy which makes him into a world within himself. If he desires union with another person, then it is only a surplus. This, according to Kermode, is the crux of the romantic image, romance being a state of self-containment, being a whole, being a Being.

1 Frank Kermode. The Romantic Image. Routledge. Published as Classics. UK. 2002. Pp 72-75.

We have observed that Amitabh is better paired with his male co-stars because they help him in achieving the inner unity while the relationship with women were surplus that took place outside the unity he achieved within him. Amitabh's erotica was always in excess of the basic constitution of his personality.[2]

Perhaps this is why, while Rajesh Khanna personified the song, Amitabh Bachchan personified the dance. As Kermode writes, Yeats says that dance integrates the opposites, rhythm is about a beat and its absence, the constant dissolve of movement into stillness, of the high pitch into the low tone, merging together movements from the opposite directions.

---

2 Martin Heidegger. Being and Time. Harper and Row. New York, 1962. Republished Harperperennial. New York. 2008, Pg 131

The Lethal Image of the Hero

The image of Amitabh Bachchan, notwithstanding his great many admirers, has something overwhelming, something intimidating, and something dangerous, lethal and even downright villainous about him. There is a kind of unpredictability that surrounds his persona; one never knows when he will stab you in the back and change camps. There are always doubts over whether he is honest or manipulative, or whether he is faithful or adulterous. There is a certain kind of secrecy about the persona of Amitabh Bachchan; people still think that he is hiding his affair with Rekha and has a very shady parallel life of sexual adventures.

There is a streak of spite in him; he may be unscrupulous and conspiring, he may be vindictive and scheming. No wonder he did so well in the film *Don* in which Don was such a man. Rajesh Khanna believed till his very last day that Amitabh had done something to his career in order to delist him as the reigning superstar of the Hindi film industry, and the gossip has it that Amitabh also played a part in driving out Vinod Khanna to his exile in Rajneesh's Ashram. Interestingly, Parveen Babi also fled to a monastic order while she was with Amitabh Bachchan on a series of stage shows abroad. These stories when added up, create a rather manipulative image of Amitabh Bachchan, which in the popular mind, is intrinsic to the superstar. Her accusations against Amitabh Bachchan, though done in a fit of schizophrenia, nonetheless put into words the extreme maneuverings which Amitabh is imagined to be capable of.

People have considered Amitabh as miserly and uncharitable, ungrateful and an opportunist, and one who never acknowledges the good deeds of the others. This is vindicated in the way he has lost close friends like Amjad Khan, Shatrughan Sinha, Kader Khan and even his Godfather Mehmood. Salim Khan complains that Amitabh has not acknowledged his role in making him into a superstar; Hrishikesh Mukherjee thinks him to be narrow minded and selfish and competitive; his portrayal of Amitabh in *Abhiman* and *Jurmana* were not too complimentary.

Interestingly, Amitabh Bachchan has always been associated with everything that is big. When the Meridian Hotel was built in Delhi in the early 1980's, the rumour was that it belonged to Amitabh Bachchan. When the Bofors deal was signed, the press accused him of having commissioned the deal, ignoring the fact that the Bofors guns have been a part of the Indian weaponry for times much before Amitabh Bachchan. Even after his bankruptcy and financial ruin, people believe that Amitabh Bachchan means the biggest haul. The association of superlatives with the hero is an attribute of his image.

Why is lethality and largeness both parts of the essence of Amitabh Bachchan? I think that the way his image is constructed has something to do with it. Amitabh Bachchan's image is a series of opposites; there is unyielding atheism in *Deewar* as well as complete surrender to God in *Amar Akbar Anthony*, the hero has no idea of his past in *Zanjeer* and is wholly aware of the same in *Deewar*. In *Zanjeer*, he is the law keeper; in *Deewar*, he attacks the law keeper. In Manmohan Desai's films, the hero is a comedian, in many films like *Adalat*, *Andha Kanoon* and *Aakhri Raasta*, mirth seems to have abandoned him. He is an ascetic and a teetotaler in *Desh Premee*, and an alcoholic in *Sharaabi*. Total restraint and full abandon, uncompromising rebellion and passive acceptance of fate are equally the part of the same image. Yet it is not as if

Amitabh's image achieved all of these by acting over a variety of roles across a body of films; in fact, at every moment, in each of his roles, the opposites are contained in every gesture of the hero. The image is therefore always dialectic, inwardly tense, and develops, due to the inner tension, a kind of a potential force ready to be unleashed with great might if allowed unrestrained release. To my mind, the holding together of opposing forces within the image at every moment gives the idea of the great power of the hero. The power to hold together opposites at all times and to be able to bear such high pressure may have made minds of his viewers imagine his lethality.

The imagination of Amitabh Bachchan as being lethal by the people is perhaps due to an asymmetry of power, a power which resides not only in the body but also in the mind, especially a mind which could conceptualise action till its final fruition. While it is easy enough to grasp the action of the body, it is difficult for most to grasp the inner workings of the mind and the mind that engenders the fantastic action through acute observations, focused reflection, measured planning and meticulous execution. This makes the image of Amitabh Bachchan as one who stands head and shoulders in intelligence over the others. This high intelligence is perhaps the reason why people cannot often grasp the mind of Amitabh Bachchan and indeed, his lethality stems more from the mind than from the body. Amitabh's lethality is not imagined in terms of his commanding an army of goons, or he is imagined to conspire and strategise.

Amitabh seems to be capable of everything. He is capable of spying into the most private spaces and he is also seen as being capable of flying high in the most powerful circle of politics. This capability perhaps comes from the various roles he essayed in which he can operate almost everywhere and under every kind of challenge. Amitabh's family background as one in which he used to be connected to the top political family, namely Nehru Gandhis, and that too with such closeness, also may have added to his image of lethality. In the days of Rajiv Gandhi's Prime Ministership, Amitabh Bachchan was often assumed to be the shadow ruler of the country, when every decision and every policy was manipulated, especially to suit his interest.

Amitabh Bachchan invokes superlatives like megastar, the biggest, the largest, richest, and the most influential, the most powerful, lethal, most dangerous, and extremely manipulative and so on. These seem to suggest that Amitabh's image had a kind of an aggregation and then an abstraction. It has been discussed in an earlier essay that Amitabh's image in *Deewar* was created out of both *Mother India* as well as *Ganga Jumna*; similarly, he has absorbed Mehmood, Asrani, Dilip Kumar, and even many shades of Shakespearan characters, perhaps in his days doing theatre. But he has totally kept out Raj Kapoor, Dev Anand, Ashok Kumar, Rajendra Kumar or Rajesh Khanna. I think that Amitabh Bachchan's aggregation have been more of sentiments and emotions; he seems to have collected a great many emotions from across the Hindi film and then abstracted these into his own expressions. For instance, he seems to have incorporated both the father and son from *Mughal E Azam*, otherwise he could not have done his role in *Deewar*, or *Kala Paththar* or even *Trishul* and *Kabhie Kabhie*. He has absorbed the sentiments of Dilip Kumar, Manoj Kumar and Sunil Dutt, otherwise he could not have pulled off *Khoon Pasina* or *Ganga Ki Saugandh*. He must have punched the essence of Rajendra Kumar and Dilip Kumar very well for his performance in *Muqaddar Ka Sikandar*. I see a lot of Waheeda Rehman's emotions in the last mentioned film as well. I see a lot of Rekha in *Desh Premee* and even in *Do Anjaane* and *Alaap* in which they work opposite each other. I see Hema Malini of *Seeta Aur Geeta* in his role in *Lawaaris*.

At the discursive level, when he argues against the system, its police and the law; when he defends his behaviour that the entrenched society looks upon as unlawful, I think that he combines the feelings of Raj Kapoor of *Awara*, Dev Anand of *Kala Pani*, Dilip Kumar in *Naya Daur*, Guru Dutt in *Pyasa*, Manoj Kumar in *Purab Aur Paschim*, and Prithviraj Kapoor in *Sikandar* and *Mughal e Azam*. He abstracts from a whole lot of discourses, absorbs them, and presents them as one aggregated whole. In this way, he touches the limits of whatever has ever been said and done in the Hindi films. Herein, perhaps lies the mystery of Amitabh Bachchan being always referred to in superlatives. The lethality also comes from the superlative epithets.

The Formula of a Star

Stars are Located in Popular Culture

The idea of Amitabh Bachchan must start with the idea of a star. The definition of a star varied in accordance to the times; in mediaeval Central Asia, they were Hamza Amir and storytellers like him; in the 16th century India, saints like Meera bai and Baiju Bawra were stars; during the freedom struggle, they were the freedom fighters and in independent India, the stars are mainly produced in popular cinema and in cricket. Stars are protagonists, individuals who produce the popular culture; politics may well be popular culture in times of great transformations like in freedom movements, or in great revolutions. John Fiske says that popular culture is unstructured and loose and through its state of looseness, can easily enter the everyday lives of the people who consume it.[1]

Games as Metaphors of Life

Stars in India are produced out of the popular cinema and cricket, and both are tightly structured, and they have become the metaphors of the lives of people in independent India. For Latin America, football is their national metaphor, for China, Japan

1 John Fiske. Understanding Popular Culture. Routledge. Taylor and Francis. South Asian Edition. London and New York. 2009.Pg 133.

and much of Eastern Europe, it is gymnastics; for America, it is baseball and for India, it is cricket that is seen to be structured around the principle of life itself. The batsman plays alone in a field of attack and being literally trapped by 11 men of the opponent team where he, together with a partner at the other end of the wicket, must score his runs. The protagonist of the popular cinema is like a cricketer, one who plays in terms of the rules of the game; not collectively but individually as a lone batsman facing the onslaught of a bowler and the resistance of a set of fielders spread out in unexpected points in a closed and defined field area; the game is played against a definite set or rules to which all players must adhere to. Cricket in India is a metaphor of life itself and the cinema too, like cricket, is the abstract rendition of life whose rules are constituted through social values, norms, expectations and aspirations.

Formulaic Structure of Popular Cinema

Stars are difficult to be created until and unless there is a clear formula. Since popular culture is directed to reorder people's cognition, culture, meaning systems, values, sentiments, rationality and even philosophical systems, it must have a system of its own, and because it challenges the establishments and the institutions of its times, it has to have an order. The formula is that order. Popular culture is formulaic.

The popular cinema is formulaically structured to resemble the everyday life of an ordinary person in the ordinary business of life, where the protagonist wants to lead a normal life of family, children, parents, friends, and a minimum level of dignity. Popular cinema, irrespective of the language it is made in, has a core structure, which is fairly universal across India, and while they differ in flavour from one another depending on regional specificities, in an overall manner, they deal with goals of ordinary men and women in the ordinariness of everyday life. The protagonist pursues goals of an ordinary person in the ordinary business of life; s/he is neither an adventurer, nor a scientist, not even a political leader, and indeed till very recently, biopics were not a part of the Indian popular cinema. The drama of life appears as the drama of the cinema in which the protagonist finds herself in situations in which s/he has to overcome quite a few barriers that deny her or him the basic necessities. These barriers appear in the form of characters in the society, mainly depicted through stereotypes known as stock characters, the jealous relative, the greedy uncle, the lustful boyfriend, the scheming manager, the cruel father, the wronged mother, the helpless sister, difficult brother and so on.

It is not enough to say that the popular cinema extols the social values; for the popular cinema must show a way to its audience to fulfil their aspirations as well. John Fiske says that popular culture is contradictory; at one level it resists the power structures, while at another, it nurtures and upholds the status quo.[2]

In order to understand what the conservative aspects of popular culture are and which aspects constitute the resistance to powers, we must delve into the constitution of the Indian society in its moments of producing popular cinema.

The Hindi Cinema has Changed over Time

The cinema started in India as early as it started in much of the first world of the colonisers. The innovativeness of the Indians, the eagerness to handle this new technology, the richness of its culture and the acute politics of decolonisation, all contributed to the development of the cinema. The star emerged around the 1930's, a period when idea of what the new Indian society would look like after Independence, was beginning to be formed through literature, drama, theatre, education and above all, through its Gandhian politics of mass movements against the British. The freedom struggle was as much of a cultural movement as much as it was political, and while a part of it was indeed against the British, but most of it was emancipatory,

2 John Fiske. Understanding Popular Culture. Routledge. Taylor and Francis. South Asian Edition. London. 2009. Pg 49.

a desire for a society deeply stratified and structured with various levels of oppressions of caste and gender, of class and community to emerge from these oppressions. Individualism was not so much of an exercise of agency in order to bring about changes in industry, science or technology as had been in Europe, but to merely rise above the social oppressions and be as equal as anyone else to beget the dignity to live life most ordinarily without the oppressions of social traditions and the weights of the stratified order. No wonder democracy thrives so truly in India; rather surprising for a nation of illiterate and poor majority which is linguistically, culturally and religion wise so diverse.

Star as Individualism in Democracy Seeking Equality

The uniting thread of India is its pursuit of individualism, where every person seeks to overcome the social oppression in order to live life conservatively in terms of those very social values which had given rise to the stratification in the first place. India's aspirations are oxymoronic; everyone wants to inhere the age-old traditional values but no one wants to be at the receiving end of those values; it amounts to saying that no one criticises oppression because everyone wants to appear as the oppressor. The danger of such a thought process may sometimes lead to the spread of a culture which creates the aspirations to become the oppressors as the only way out of being the oppressed, a typical phenomenon of fascism – the Hindi film has been mercilessly criticised for this.

Masculine and Feminine as Stars

The star of the popular cinema is therefore the ordinary person in the ordinary business of life who must reflect the aspirations of living life ordinarily; what is exceptional in him/her is how s/he overcomes the social structures that prevent her/him from leading the life of aspirations. But what are her aspirations? Not much beyond marrying for love, earn to live and look after the ailing mother or raise a child and to fight for the restoration of honour of a wronged father or a raped sister. There are differences between a male star and a female star, though, a female star is more concerned with marriage and raising her children while the men are more concerned about livelihoods and fighting for honour. The female star is all about the life within the private sphere of marriage and reproduction while the male star engages more with the public space of life opportunities and social entitlements in terms of livelihood and honour. Within the strictly- defined formula of the cinema, stars do differ from one another in terms of their personality traits, attitude towards life, address and aggregation of experiences and in their theory of obstacles that stand in the way of their self-fulfilment.

Stars are Actors with Authorial Tendencies

Stars are created by writers and placed on screen by directors, actors have to merely perform out the script. If so, then why would the star be so important? Stars are important precisely because of the physical body which they lend to present the script to the viewer and it is here that the actor makes a crucial transformation by taking what is merely written and imagined as a frame of a film into an activity of the body. Stars are not merely actors for they do not, unlike very fine actors, delve deep into roles and become the persons they act as; stars, on the other hand, usually play a unique persona, emerging as quite the same person across the roles they play. The films they act in become various situations presented to them and they emerge with greater number of attributes added to their persona as if through the many trials which they go through in the form of the roles.

The Formula of a Star

We must spend some more time to reflect upon the question, of how an actor becomes a star, or for that matter, how any individual become a star? To my mind, stars are not mere performers, they perform with a level of cognitive integration in their minds. In other words, individuals who perform not merely tasks but have a holistic idea about the work that they do, their roles in it, clear pictures about how the world should like, idea of how to engage themselves in the making of that world. Stars generate ideas and implement, are teachers and guides, inspirational performers and exemplars. Stars are popular figures rather than performers of tasks; the star belongs to the popular consciousness becoming a manner of thought, mode of behaviour, a way of perceiving and a world view.

Raj Kapoor versus Amitabh Bachchan

Raj Kapoor and Amitabh Bachchan are both stars who defined their own eras. Raj Kapoor is of course a producer and a director as well and the owner of studios. Raj Kapoor is really not merely a star; he is an establishment and the one who ruled over the entire transformation of the formula-driven popular Hindi film from the pre-Independence to the post-Independence days. Amitabh Bachchan is a star who could never successfully emerge into the business of filmmaking and was financially ruined in trying to set up an entertainment company. Amitabh remains an individual performer while Raj Kapoor is an institution. A comparison between the two would be unfair. Yet, as stars, one must compare the two, not to privilege one over the other, but to seek out the traits within Amitabh Bachchan, the assignment at hand.

Let us take *Awara* made in 1951 starring Raj Kapoor and *Deewar* made in 1975, starring Amitabh Bachchan as examples. Both films were about protagonists abandoned by their respective fathers, when both were immensely attached to their mothers. Both heroes turn against the law if only as a means to survive in the world, and both find father figures in the underworld. Both heroes enter into an argumentative conflict with the law; in *Awara*, Raj Kapoor is sent to prison by his father who is the judge, and in *Deewar*, Amitabh Bachchan is shot down by his brother who is a policeman. Both films constituted the basic text of the respective stars.[1]

There are major differences between the two stars. Raj Kapoor remains a child at heart, despite the fact that he leaves school and enters into the working world to fend for his mother just as Amitabh did in *Deewar*. Raj Kapoor is sentimental about his existence and emotional in his actions while Amitabh gulps down his sentiments, and even though emotions are the well of his actions; yet he brushes these aside to avenge the world. Raj Kapoor flows with the world; content remaining in his station of life and busy with survival. Amitabh has already survived in the first third of the film and after that he goes about with the 'surplus', trying to build an empire out of his angst and experiences, out of his sense of justice and to consummate his ideas of a just world. Amitabh's roles are never mere responses to situations, for he resolves his problems and moves much ahead to establish his ideas upon the world in order to order and transform it.

In *Awara*, Raj Kapoor's anchor is Rita, the beautiful girl brought up by Raj's father. This is Nargis, Raj Kapoor's heroine in the best of his films, who he called the 'mother of his cinema'. Nargis is Raj Kapoor's anchor throughout the film and in *Deewar*, though Amitabh Bachchan lives in with Parveen Babi, who plays the bar dancer; yet the centre of Amitabh's life remains the mother, and after that, the child that Parveen Babi is expecting. The erotic romance serves little purpose precisely because as a hero, Amitabh is a loner who absorbs everything within him, ruminates by himself and collapses inwardly like a black hole. Raj Kapoor is an expressionist, bringing all that is within him into the display of the bright lights of cinema. This is why, in the final scene when Raj is behind the bars, he says that he is happy because within the prison, he is safer than he is in the world outside. For him, the law is protection. Between the state and the

1 Star names rather than the character names are used for easy reading

society, Raj Kapoor raises a case invoking the State to protect the individual against the society.

For Amitabh Bachchan in *Deewar*, the law is oppression and he dies surrendering to the law. Of course the state must protect the citizen who does not own arms against the miscreants who own arms, because the State alone has the monopoly of force. But like the villains, the State also uses force against those individuals who act on behalf of the State when the State fails to do its duty. In *Deewar* and all across Amitabh's films, there is an innate desire for the individual to become the State, especially as when the State fails to discharge its duties.

Raj Kapoor is a citizen, Amitabh is the State. Raj Kapoor is all about sentiments, Amitabh is about the law. Raj Kapoor loves to return to his loved ones; Amitabh bears the sorrow of having lost them.

Dev Anand and Amitabh Bachchan

Dev Anand is an important star to reckon with because he was supposed to play the lead in *Zanjeer*, the film that established Amitabh Bachchan in his role as the angry young man of India. Javed Akhtar, Javed of the Salim Javed duo, writers who invented the angry young man image of Amitabh Bachchan, was a fan of Dev Anand, and it was with the imagination of the star in his mind that he, with Salim Khan, wrote the script of *Zanjeer*. But Dev Anand refused and the role was offered to Dharmendra, and when the latter refused as well, it was the relative new comer with only a string of flop films behind him who was selected for the lead role.[1] In the shades which Amitabh brought to the character of Vijay, interestingly, Dev Anand did not even cast a shadow. I personally do not believe in the story of *Zanjeer* being written for Dev Anand.

The story of *Zanjeer* revolves around an orphan who sees his parents being shot dead by someone. He is unable to see the murderer's face but catches a glimpse of the hand in which he holds the revolver and from it slings a bracelet with a pendant of a horse. The investigating officer adopts the orphan and raises

1 Soumya Bandopadhyay. Amitabh Bachchan. (Bengali) Ananda Publishers. Kolkata. 1995.

him as his own son and the child grows up to be a police officer. The story is then all about finding the murderer and avenging the murder of his parents. But here is the tricky bit: because Vijay barely remembers the murder, he has almost no memory of his parents, and in all probability, does not recall the murderer at all; he is only disturbed by a dream of a cloaked man riding a white horse which comes to haunt him even in his waking hours. The mental agony moves him, albeit unconsciously makes him cruel towards criminals. For purposes of comparing Amitabh Bachchan and Dev Anand, we may choose the latter's film, *Kala Pani*, in which the hero decides to reopen an old case buried and gone, in order to release his father from prison where he is sentenced for life. The hero of *Kala Pani* knows his father, is aware of the mission and actively pursues the investigation.

Dev Anand plays the protagonist called Karan and is a man without any doubt about his goals, his own abilities and his mission. Amitabh, playing the role of Vijay, is a man who has an inner calling but which he is yet to articulate in the lived world. Vijay has two layers; one is the fulfilment of a goal but the other is also to find that goal. Karan is free of doubt and his body language is confident and relaxed; he finds time for some laughter and mirth, he flirts and romances, he investigates and enjoys life despite the fact that before he started on his journey, he was quite an emotional wreck. Vijay, Amitabh's character in *Zanjeer*, stiff and taciturn, holds himself tightly and tautly, bottles up his emotions which effervesces only in lethal fights with villains, he is ever alert to the level of being jumpy, and has no time to spare on the fineries of life such as song, dance and romance.

Dev Anand's actions confirmed his urbanity, the suaveness of his persona and it was as if he was trying to establish his elegance through the movie. Amitabh was not supposed to be an urban person but the sophistication that he inherited through his upbringing, education and employment gave him his metrosexual polish. With this inherent city-bred style, Amitabh, as the hero, encountered a world which could only dishevel him, dirty him; the more he engaged in fights and the more layers of his veneer he shed, the more urbane and sophisticated he was revealed at the core.

Dev Anand did not need to be a fighter, for fights could unsettle his bedecked demeanour; but Amitabh fought to lose his demeanour, the shearing off, the lessening and hence the unburdening, became an emancipatory experience for his followers. Dev Anand is cerebral; Amitabh is philosophical and even spiritual because of his open acceptance of the uncertainties that he faces. Dev Anand appears forever to be above things; it is as if his battles are already won. Amitabh needs to be forever in the process of fighting, for even in the scenes where Amitabh is not fighting, moments build up towards a fight. Dev Anand provides steady state entertainment; Amitabh provides a heady state of drama.

Both, Dev Anand and Amitabh Bachchan are lonesome figures; Dev Anand is often seen retiring by himself all alone, withdrawn from the world. In case of Amitabh, he is always lonesome, though sometimes he may attend a musical jamboree to unwind; solitude is Amitabh's natural state of being which sometimes undergoes a change of scene at parties on screen.

Dev Anand's image is that of Casanova, a flirt, and a playboy, and this image was constantly protected and even reinforced by his actions on screen. For Amitabh, this was just the opposite; he would give up his image, abandon what he started off with, obliterate his entitlements, and erase traces of his legacy, and in this loss of disposition, the scope of his activities increased limitlessly.

Dilip Kumar and Amitabh Bachchan

Dilip Kumar and Amitabh Bachchan appear to have an uneasy relationship. Jaya Bachchan, Amitabh's wife, openly says that no one can be a better actor than Dilip Kumar, thus seemingly favouring the thespian to her superstar husband.[1] People say and with a lot of truth that Amitabh copies Dilip Kumar in his acting style. Dilip Kumar has often shown a tongue in cheek appreciation of Amitabh Bachchan; the latter has praised the thespian in empty words. During the shooting of *Shakti*, Dilip Kumar rather sarcastically called out to the crowds to be quiet because 'Amitabh Bachchan' was rehearsing his scenes.[2] Both actors are famous for their tragedies; Dilip Kumar's image seems to logically culminate in tragedy; Amitabh's image is tragic despite his many victories. Dilip Kumar is fulfilled when tragic; Amitabh is tragic because despite his successes, he is never fulfilled.

Dilip Kumar's image is best viewed in *Devdas* in which he absorbs his sorrow inside him till the point it totally destroys him; his emotions are far too much for him to express and he collapses under the weight of his emotions. In *Muquaddar ka Sikandar*, Amitabh's version of *Devdas*, the hero chooses to die, for he could

1 https://www.youtube.com/watch?v=oqJ_KVtR4yw&t=214s
2 https://www.youtube.com/watch?v=ua-jRgtqNwA

well have expressed his love for the lady but chooses, instead, to hold himself back. There is once again an exercise of choice, and unlike Dilip Kumar in *Devdas*, where emotions stalled his actions, Amitabh's portrayal of Sikandar was one where actions consciously brushed off ineffable emotions.

Devdas has been made many times by different actors in Hindi as well as in regional languages. It is perhaps the most remade film ever. But every actor has brought his nuances into the role of Devdas. K.L.Saigal brings grandeur and ego in the role, Shah Rukh Khan brings obsession and paints the character in shades of narcissism, and Dilip Kumar concentrates every kind of emotion into the role as if Devdas were a compendium of bottled up passions that inhered the totality of life. Amitabh's character Sikandar is one of self-command and self-control, one who is stoked by intense passion for his lady love but decides not to cross his limits because he was once her servant. The appeal of Sikandar lies in the hero's conscious command over his passions, swallowing his feelings, silencing his heart and choosing death so that his love is never expressed.

It is interesting because Dilip Kumar has been the quintessential son; subjugated by parental authority, hurt by discipline and irked by demands of conformity to social norms, and Amitabh's image is quintessentially that of the father with self-control, self-discipline and of self-authority, rather than being a person who receives command. This is why, the film *Shakti* is so anomalous because Dilip Kumar played the father and Amitabh, the son. If by some freak of nature, were the roles to be reversed, *Shakti* could have been one of the finest marks left on Hindi cinema. Indeed, *Mughal-e-Azam*, in which the thespian played the role of Salim, Emperor Akbar's rebellious son and heir to the throne, is one of the finest works of the star. Amitabh has easily slipped into roles of elderly characters as the attributes of the father was imprinted upon him, while Dilip Kumar's elderly roles have not been remarkable.

Dilip Kumar's withdrawn emotions create spaces for his female co-stars to shine through on screen. Javed Akhtar says of

Dilip Kumar that he had a 'way of looking' at his women, as if his lady would become more and more beautiful were he to regard her visually. This is a fete he could accomplish by a strategy of withholding emotions and the more he withheld expression, the more expressive his face would become. The world of Dilip Kumar seems so much like a vacuum in which his emotions do not find suitable media to travel, and hence, escapes bodilessly as if in space, to inhere the whole of the film material. Casting Dilip Kumar must have been difficult for the directors because not only the frames in which the actor appears but the entire montage had to be designed in order to accommodate the emotional flavour of the actor.

Amitabh Bachchan's expression of emotions were different for the principle reason that the spring well of his emotions were not related to romance, and even when he pined for unrequited love, such as in *Kabhie Kabhie*, these would transform frequently to concern for the family and instead of withholding, he actively killed or mutated his romantic inclinations within himself. He often lets go of his romantic interests and focusses instead on his family and with issues of earning a livelihood. This is why the film *Silsila* is such a surprise, and it whetted the appetite of a public, hungry for pure romance from Amitabh Bachchan. Gossips around Amitabh's affair mainly with Rekha and other co-stars like Parveen and Zeenat Aman have rocked the press over decades, perhaps because Amitabh's image, both in real and in reel life, was that of a family man, uncorrupted by the lure of romance outside of the family.

Guru Dutt and Amitabh Bachchan

It is a bit strange to compare Guru Dutt and Amitabh Bachchan, especially since Amitabh seems to always win and Guru Dutt is always losing on screen and perhaps in real life as well. Yet, one can compare the two, for both prove through the evidence of their lives, the anomalies of the society, belie of promises by the establishment, the oppression of the systems and the orders which contains the lives of humans and gives their actions and experiences some meaning. Both address the macro economy, the State, the politics and the ways of the society as a whole, rather than the vices of some bad humans. For both, their troubles are not personal but systemic.

Both Guru Dutt and Amitabh live in the city; Amitabh has been set against a village in *Saudagar* and *Desh Premee* but on the whole,like Guru Dutt, he too is a city guy. The anomalies they face are not contingent or fortuitous but structural and institutional, and these emerge from social processes underway. The city is the outcome of deep social transitions and hence it becomes the source of hostility. Guru Dutt in *Pyasa* and Amitabh in *Deewar* and then many more of such films, both are anomalies of the city life, precisely because the city which is supposed to be the space of social opportunities and higher level of civilisation is fraught with mistrust, betrayals, cheatings and above all, of marginalisation due to downright poverty. Guru Dutt and Amitabh are similar to each other in presenting the city as a state of human despair rather than of redemption.

The difference between the two is that Guru Dutt is defeated in the city, Amitabh emerges victorious in it, rich, wealthy, vindicated and finally honoured. Amitabh conquers the city, Guru Dutt is conquered in the city. The city for both is hopeless, a haven of opportunism rather than being a place where hope is kindled and opportunities lie. The city sharpens the class divides among people and every moment reminds one of one's lack of social entitlements.

Pyasa's Gulabo perhaps becomes Anita in *Deewar*, both dancing girls who balm the hero in their respective dark days; Gulabo saves Guru Dutt, Anita dooms the hero. In Guru Dutt's films, despite the desperation of the city, the feminine principle emerges as the redeemer; for Amitabh's films, the feminine is the resident evil.

Shammi Kapoor and Amitabh Bachchan

The little that I have seen Amitabh and Shammi together I sensed that Shammi held a slightly imposing attitude over Amitabh and that would make the latter engage in defensive and argumentative conversations. Shammi would use a sentence here and there to rile him in, often casting sidelong glances at others to assess the effect he was having in needling the megastar. Amitabh had not only usurped the position of all stars but he had also taken away from Shammi the epithet of being the game changer. Amitabh was the game changer and such a game changer he was that the Hindi film industry can be imagined as a pre, a post and of course an Amitabh Bachchan era, during which the cinema changed story wise, feel wise and above all, commercially. Shammi Kapoor changed the idea of the body of the star by dancing vigorously while Amitabh Bachchan changed the idea of the body by fighting valiantly, running hard and performing difficult stunts, often by himself. Deleuze says that cinema is nothing but movement and the movement is best when it inheres in the body.[1] If the actor can move well and faster than the rest of the actors, cinematic text inclines towards him/her and everything in the film narrative rises in the form of a montage

1 Gilles Deleuze. Cinema 1. Continuum. South Asian Edition. 1986. Pg 1

to support the actor with movement. In short, the actor with the most movement commands the most attention in the cinema. Movement of the body is a way of gaining not just stardom but superstardom as well. Both Shammi and Amitabh concentrated a lot of movement into them.

However, Amitabh's movements were not merely of the body but those of the mind as well. By holding emotions back instead of expressing them, by absorbing experiences and connecting them together, then emerging with a critique of the system, the hero's aggressions were both intellectual and moral as well as bodily. Amitabh's actions emanated from deep reflection and were not merely physical feats. This is why, those who thought that one could rise to the level of Amitabh by fighting very hard like Akshay Kumar and Ajay Devgan could hardly reach Amitabh's levels because the action was the end state of a prolonged rumination and not merely a bodily enactment. More recent films like *Sarkar, Wazir and Te3n* showed how Amitabh, despite his age, disability and bereavement was still the action hero and thus vindicate the thesis that action is more in the mind, in the mind's vision of achieving a goal, of changing one's situation.

Using the schemata of Deleuze, we may say that Shammi Kapoor's action is the small frame action while that of Amitabh's the large scale action. Deleuze says that a person with the large frame action acts upon a situation to change it, the formula being S1-A-S2, S1 and S2 are the two situations changed on account of the action A. The actor of the large frame conceives of action based on his or her reading of the different situations. The actor of the small frame is described by Deleuze as A1-S-A2, in which the actor acts upon the situation S and changes his or her activity levels.[2] The actor of the small scale is an actor who acts out of habit, because of a certain level of body energy which makes him active. Shammi Kapoor represents the small frame very well; expressing his body energy appears to be his goal. For Amitabh, it is a thought process, a philosophy which gets translated into action, the action rides on physicality but is not physical.

---

2 Gilles Deleuze. ibid. Pp 164-167.

Sunil Dutt and Amitabh Bachchan

The mother, son and the absent father was possibly a theme that the writers, Salim Khan and Javed Akhtar, took from Mehboob Khan's film, *Mother India*, for their ground breaking work in *Deewar*. *Mother India*, a film written and directed by Mehboob Khan in 1957, was principally the search for the ideal Indian woman, loyal to husband, immune to temptations, stoic to sufferrings, stern towards wilful abandon, and one who can raise her children with honesty and integrity all by herself. The absent father is helpful to bring out the ideals in a woman for child bearing and child rearing are both supposed to be hers. The Indian male is notorious for not taking care of household chores and child-rearing responsibilities and the absence of the father also becomes a way of absolving the male of all duties in the private space. *Deewar* strongly reverses this and despite the valiant fights of the hero with villains in the anonymity of the city, he is the one who is essentially concerned about the home, to protect it, to bring food to the table, to rear and nurture it. The hero, played by Amitabh, takes in the maternal functions, and in a man becoming his own parents, reduces his wife to the periphery; romance therefore becomes routinised and sometimes even extraneous in Amitabh's films.

Vijay in *Deewar* and Birju in *Mother India* are supposed to be corresponding roles; one wonders whether Vijay was also not another form of Birju. While Vijay means victory, Birju is a nickname for bravery. Birju in *Mother India* is like Raju in *Awara*; innocent and naïve, metamorphosing from adolescence to adulthood. For Vijay, anywhere he appears, for Amitabh has usually been called as Vijay, seems as if born an adult. He is transformed into an adult very early in life and never seems to have a childhood; he moves instead, into death. In *Mother India*, Birju dies killed by his own mother as a disciplinary action and in *Deewar*, Vijay dies as well, killed by his brother, but instigated by his mother, which is also an execution of sorts. The killing in Mother India is impulsive, spontaneous and reactionary while in *Deewar*, the killing is planned and reasoned. Nothing in Amitabh's films appear as innocent and spontaneous; things are always planned and directed. Amitabh's films are dominated by reason, Sunil Dutt's films are dominated by will. This is why, despite very similar roles that each play, they seem quite contrary to each other. One of Amitabh's earlier breaks was in a film called *Reshma Aur Shera*, written and directed by Sunil Dutt, in which Sunil Dutt plays the lead role, Shera. Amitabh Bachchan, known for his baritone and exact articulation, was rendered silent in the film as he played a dumb character. Both Sunil Dutt and Amitabh Bachchan were close to the Nehru family and Mrs Indira Gandhi, and both have been Members of Parliament.

Birju is by his mother's side but never takes over his mother's centrality; but Vijay in *Deewar* takes over his mother's worries and takes over the role of the bread winner. While Vijay always thinks of retiring his mother into comfort, Birju always thinks of being by his mother' side, close to her and please her by bringing in what she lacks. Amitabh always takes entire control of things, straddles the screen and towers over every other character, paling them in his comparison; perhaps this is why in the due course of his career, Amitabh's films became louder, more garish and highly exaggerated, as if to overcome the ennui of having to see only a single face on screen.

One reads a lot in books about how Amitabh Bachchan was the epitome of masculinity in his films. So was Sunil Dutt, because all the dacoit roles belonged to him in a near monopoly. Sunil Dutt's masculinity was all brawn; a constant struggle between lust and love in which the more refined emotions seemed to compromise his masculinity. Amitabh's masculinity was perhaps beyond sexuality, for he remained masculine despite loving his children and missing his mother. Amitabh's masculinity entered somewhat an asexual zone, in which the hero dispensed with the need of the feminine to complement him. The uncoupling of the feminine and the masculine within his body, raising it to the level of asceticism, constituted Amitabh's masculinity. Sunil Dutt's masculinity is adolescent while Amitabh's is elegant.

Rajesh Khanna and Amitabh Bachchan

While I was working on Amitabh Bachchan, I sensed a need to understand Rajesh Khanna well because it was important to understand the phenomenon of the superstar as a generic concept. If Amitabh Bachchan was angry with the world, Rajesh Khanna was its redeemer. The latter's image was one that constituted the fantasy of women for, when they are caught in the mires of misfortune of life, and become lonely, bereft and even homeless, there comes Rajesh Khanna to elevate their souls. It is to such women that Rajesh Khanna emerges as an emancipator, freeing them often from themselves and of course from their milieu. No wonder then women would go berserk with Rajesh Khanna. If the cinema is all about movement, then the persona of Rajesh Khanna constitutes a movement in cinema of unprecedented scale. He is best placed in open spaces, upon moving trains, often against vast valleys and gushing mountain streams, or on a boat afloat a wide river. He sails in resembling the wind that blows softly to fill up the entire visible space. Rajesh Khanna has been able to align his body movements and his facial expressions against this space and movement. His own bodily movements are small and measured as if to tickle the universe in which he prevails. He does not appear to be of the world, seeming to remain above the ground, in the ether, some other worldly presence who comes visiting by your window, bringing in your life the song of some vista as yet unexplored. When he moves, he pulls the viewer with him, and the movement is transported from the body of the star into the body of the viewer; Rajesh Khanna changes the entire scale of movement.

In contrast to Rajesh Khanna, Amitabh's movements are ground level, earthy, palpable and tactile. He engaged with the world, fought with blood and gore, emerged from the mud and grime, blood and sweat. If Rajesh Khanna redeemed trapped women, Amitabh tried to extricate himself from his being trapped into the world's oppressive and exploitative system. Amitabh is not an illusion, his is a life where dreams turn into nightmares, fears haunt him and even when he rescues his mother and fiancée, friend or brother, he is basically redeeming himself; these are challenges that he has taken up for himself. In *Deewar,* he fights Peter because he has murdered Nandu; Nandu is an excuse for the hero to fight Peter, because in that fight, he will reverse the helplessness against physical violence to which his father was subjected to in the past.

Rajesh Khanna's concern is not with himself, for he is already liberated. His concern is the liberation of the heroine. In *Aradhana*, he emerges twice, once as a lover and next as the son of the heroine, fulfilling her twice respectively, as a lover and as a mother. The two images of the hero in the film are identical but the images of the heroines are vastly different. As the lover, the heroine is a confident woman riding high on the elixir of her romance, while as the widow, she is crumpled, hesitant, inhibited and devastated. It is the heroine who changes, while the hero holds himself untransformed against her. The same is the situation in *Kati Patang* in which the heroine flees home because she flees from an arranged marriage and meets the hero, Rajesh Khanna, in the home of her asylum. In this home she impersonates her friend, a widow but now dead. In effect, the heroine too is a widow. Out of the cold solitude of the widow, the hero pulls out a girl eager for love and effects a transformation in her while he remains unchanged. Rajesh Khanna's imperviousness to transformation becomes an asset for his image as a superstar, for he was the pure one, one who was not polluted with his engagements with the world.

Amitabh Bachchan's journey has been one of constant '*Agneepath*', ordeals through fire when he undergoes successive purification from a state of pollution. He starts off as an abused and oppressed person and moves towards a greater purification. Amitabh Bachchan is thus transformative, his real being lies at the end of a long journey of relentless overcoming, becoming, redeeming, maturing, becoming wiser and even ageing; his transformations concerns himself but not his heroines.

For Amitabh, death often completes him; death offends Rajesh Khanna. In *Anand* as well as in *Namak Haram*, when Rajesh Khanna dies while Amitabh Bachchan helplessly looks on, death literally takes Rajesh Khanna away from us. But in *Sholay* and *Deewar* and even in *Aakhri Raasta* and *Agneepath*, where Amitabh dies as the hero of the film, death returns the hero to his home, his home being a concept of perfection which cannot be found upon this earth, may be even to a philosophical home.

I have been to the homes of both Rajesh Khanna and Amitabh Bachchan. Rajesh lives a life of a loner, in a home with lots of empty spaces and white walls, minimalistic both in décor as well as in what he has to offer by way of laying out tea. It was as if he could disappear into his house. It was in a sense a hiding. Amitabh's home in Prateeksha used to look like the inside of a palace. Despite its simplicity, it was grand because it was simple. It was both spread out yet well-organised, an army of servants would always be ready to serve you. If Rajesh's home was meditative, Amitabh's was literally the Dewan-e-Khaas or the King's court.

Rajesh Khanna is the eternal lover whom marriage corrupts. He is unable to handle marriage in *Aap ki Kasam* and *Mera Jeevan Saathi*. In *Haathi Mere Saathi*, marriage ruins his essence; he loses himself when his father in-law shoots his pet elephant, who was his life's anchor. But Amitabh Bachchan finds anchor in marriage; in *Deewar,* he surrenders when his girlfriend is pregnant with his child and in *Zanjeer*, *Trishul*, *Kala Paththar* and even in *Don*, marriage, which is only a romance now, calms the hero down. The images of the respective stars have strange but expected similarities with their real lives in which Amitabh remains a married man in monogamy while Rajesh Khanna suffers separation, divorce and a slew of serialised relationships. This is bound to be for the star is an actor with a biography; we know that stars, more often than not, are cinematic extensions of their own selves.

When we think of these images in terms of the effect they have on the viewer, we observe that Rajesh Khanna has an expansive movement, a sublimating impact on the viewer because of his bodilessness, his levity, his softness and the feeling of weightlessness. In the case of Amitabh Bachchan, we encounter a series of bodily shocks as the hero physically is constrained, beaten up and he beats up or fights out of his confinements; Amitabh activates us bodily.

Generic Superstars-Rajesh and Amitabh Again

Rajesh Khanna was the true predecessor of Amitabh Bachchan because it was he who was named as a superstar for the first time in India. Indeed, it is said that the term 'superstar' was coined specifically for Rajesh Khanna. As Amitabh says, that even at the height of his popularity, he could never beat the madness that besieged the fans of Rajesh Khanna. Women used to pick up the dust from the tire marks of the star's car and apply it as *sindoor (vermillion)* on their foreheads. The charisma of Rajesh Khanna was short lived but intense, to a degree that no one had ever encountered before him. Amitabh Bachchan displaced Rajesh Khanna not by competing with him in a straight game but by adopting a completely opposite image. They were polar opposites of each other and represented two distinct ages, though contemporaries. The last time we saw such an inflection was with Shammi Kapoor and no wonder that Amitabh tried hard at doing a Shammi jig in the film *Bombay to Goa*. There can be no comparison between Rajesh Khanna and Amitabh Bachchan, for they were like chalk and cheese and they broke the Hindi film audience qualitatively and temporarily into two distinct ages. Rajesh Khanna epitomised the age of innocence of the Hindi films while Amitabh was the man of Paradise Lost.

Rajesh Khanna has been an imagination; a man who simply flows in, literally from nowhere, without legacy, without moorings; he is a woman's fantasy of a lover. He is bodiless, light, ethereal and illuminated. In *Aradhana*, the film that established him as the superstar, he is a face on the window of a train, a fairy-like creature who appears again as if by magic, romances and eventually impregnates the heroine and disappears into death. The death of the hero takes place out of an aircraft crash. The hero comes in again as if by magic in the form of the adult son, separated from his mother in his childhood. Cinema halls would be besieged by ecstatic clapping and whistling when Rajesh Khanna reappeared in his role as the son. The dead and the rising again theme has been repeated in many a Hindi film after *Aradhana*, trying to encash on it as a formula, but it has rarely, if ever, matched in appeal. The unreal, the impossible, the fantastic have been the core of Rajesh Khanna's appeal.

If unreality was Rajesh Khanna's appeal, then reality has been Amitabh's forte. Amitabh is so real that no shade of fantasy can be cast upon him; his heroines can hardly pin their dreams on him, for he leaves them, ignores them as he feels dissuaded from his path of erotica by duties of this world. His romances are routine and short, abrupt and perfunctory and more to keep in line with the formula of the Hindi film, so as not to break the audience's expectations. If romance is a part of the formula, and Amitabh appears to have substantially broken the formula by downplaying romance, then let us never imagine that Rajesh Khanna only moved along an age-old pattern of things, for Rajesh Khanna too changed the pattern of the Hindi film to a great deal.

Rajesh Khanna starrers were mostly about women; the man had no journey of his own; his purpose was only to relieve the drudgery of his significant others by his graceful disposition. This aspect of Rajesh Khanna was brought about by Hrishikesh Mukherjee in his film *Bawarchi*, where the hero comes out of nowhere as the cook everyone was looking forward to, but could not really conceptualise. Amitabh, on the other hand, is the one who is pained with the world, pained at the world and for who drudgery is destiny, and when Rajesh Khanna co-stars with him, the duo make a far better couple than man and woman because each one complements what the other lacks.

In *Haathi Mere Saathi*, a script that Salim Javed reworked on heavily, Rajesh Khanna was rendered into the world of work. Forced into poverty by the bad guys, the hero lands up in the streets from where he rises again. Rajesh Khanna converts it into one of the mushiest tear jerkers that ever could have been. Amitabh and Rajesh Khanna differ in their emotions as well; while the latter 'hates tears' and yet cries a lot in total empathy with his significant others, Amitabh is one who does not allow tears to well up at all, pushing them back and restraining them to consolidate into anger, with which he overpowers villains. Rajesh Khanna does not seek liberation, for he is already liberated; he has no agenda of his own and appears in flesh and blood only because he feels that people need him to liberate them. This is the story of the film *Bawarchi*. In *Anand*, he comes into the hospital as a terminally- ill patient and teaches the grand lesson to his doctor who he calls *Babumoshai*, played by Amitabh Bachchan. Amitabh feels helpless in the face of death but Rajesh Khanna, as Anand, teaches him that life and death need not be separate entities, for death is a moment of life itself and not its contradiction.

Anand touches upon a major aspect of Rajesh Khanna's image; this is an image that knows no separation, no distinction. In a sharp contrast, Amitabh Bachchan is a man who lives by separating, articulating, distinguishing and identifying, naming and defining phenomena around him. He is a man who wades through separations in search for a unity that transcends such separateness among things; it is only a search but never a convincing attainment. This perhaps explains why Rajesh Khanna was devastated when his stardom ended but Amitabh's stardom, though it has journeyed over sharp bends and tall breakers, has not ended; in him resides a search that never seems to end. Rajesh Khanna, by himself, has no entity. He gets an entity when encountering an 'other'. His charisma was most apparent against strong women leads like Sharmila Tagore and

Mumtaz. He ran out of step with Zeenat Aman, Parveen Babi and even Rekha. On the other hand, Amitabh succeeded with exactly these heroines and did badly with Sharmila Tagore, Saira Banu and Nutan. A possible reason for this could be that while all of Rajesh Khanna's heroines had a journey of their own, none of Amitabh's heroines had any. Amitabh had his own agenda, the women were supposed to fill in to those as cogs in his wheels, but Rajesh Khanna braced the women's agenda while not having a specific one himself.

The 'out-of-the-world' image of Rajesh Khanna sets him against picturesque and undulating landscapes, but the within the world image of Amitabh places him into grimy slums, gritty sites, dusty roads and into plush palaces which are usually the den of villains. The geography has something to do with the music, for in Rajesh Khanna's movies, the music becomes ethereal and pervasive, while in Amitabh's films, and music is rhythmic and bodily, lending itself to dance.

It is important now to examine whether Rajesh Khanna and Amitabh Bachchan had anything in common between them so as to merit the template of the superstar. To my mind, both stars went beyond the possession of a set of attributes and characteristics to a holistic vision of life; a definite world view which made them into a system of philosophy rather than a personality made through a mere integration of attributes. We cannot define either Rajesh Khanna or Amitabh Bachchan as good, bad, honest, scheming, clever, foolish, selfish or selfless, for they represent a consciousness which have a panoptic idea of life.

Male Co-Stars

Rishi Kapoor writes in his recently published autobiography that Amitabh Bachchan rarely, if ever, has given credit to his co-stars for his superstardom and were it not for his co-stars, he would not have been where he is. Interestingly, Amitabh Bachchan is a superstar which means that he commands sole attention in his movies and yet, he has done best when pitted with another male star. More than heroines, Amitabh's 'pair' is recalled with male supporting actors.

Amitabh Bachchan constituted an era, an era of action cinema when every film would tilt towards action. Notwithstanding a *Julie*, or a *Jai Santoshi Ma* or an *Ek Duje ke Liye*, the basic formula of the Hindi film became a wronged hero with gorgons to flay and villains to slay. Every male actor was in one way or the other conscripted into this pattern. Central to this formula was the figure of Amitabh Bachchan who everyone tried to discover and explore in his capabilities in every newer forms of action; once something was already patented by Amitabh, the lesser directors would repeat it with other heroes, but the format remained as the one that emanated out of Amitabh Bachchan. Action heroes like Shatrughan Sinha, Dharmendra and Vinod Khanna continued to be in films as stars but their stardom was best displayed when they were with Amitabh Bachchan; it was as if Amitabh was also a backdrop for most stars to flourish. The only ones who ever had a niche for themselves during the era of Amitabh were Rishi Kapoor and Mithun Chakravarty.

Vinod Khanna

Amitabh looked different with different stars. Vinod Khanna was self-composed, self-confident and smart and sort of 'contained' Amitabh. They were a glorious pair of the trio in Manmohan Desai's *Amar Akbar Anthony*. Vinod Khanna looked physically stronger, suave, successful as compared to Anthony Gonsalves, the character that Amitabh Bachchan played, and it was the former's dignity that created spaces for Amitabh to horse around a bit and be relieved of his burden of being the angry young man for some time. In *Parvarish*, also by Manmohan Desai, the roles seemed reversed; Amitabh played the self-contained confident man while Vinod Khanna was wayward, but also way too clever for Amitabh Bachchan. Amitabh-Vinod Khanna pair started with Prakash Mehra's *Hera Pheri* in 1976 and went over four major films of Amitabh that includes *Muqaddar ka Sikandar* and in all the films, Vinod Khanna appeared to restrain Amitabh's actions, and yet, in effect, concentrated them in intensity.

Shashi Kapoor

Shashi Kapoor was a well-established star when Amitabh started his career as the angry young man in *Deewar* and as always, Shashi played the role of a nice average guy who is always right. Shashi Kapoor's image worked like the median, the stabilising factor when Amitabh broke social rules and moral norms to change his social status and emerge into a more empowered state of being than what society allowed for him. When Amitabh raged as a rebel, Shashi stood on his ground of law in *Deewar*; when Amitabh thundered as an insurgent, Shashi quietly allowed him his ground in *Trishul*. Shashi brings about what is always right; Amitabh challenges what is always right and Shashi, by being the calm backdrop, allows a frame for Amitabh's fury to pour out.

Dharmendra

Dharmendra was not only an established star during the years of *Zanjeer*, *Deewar* and *Sholay*, but he was already in a makeover mode from a romantic star to a rustic action hero with a golden heart since the runaway success of Raj Khosla's award winning film in 1971, *Mera Gaon, Mera Desh*. Soon after this film, Dharmendra transformed into an action hero, notwithstanding the efforts of Hrishikesh Mukherjee, who struggled to bring Dharmendra back as middle-class intelligentsia in *Anupama* and later in *Chupke Chupke*. Paired with Hema Malini, Dharmendra scaled new heights in *Jugnu* and *Seeta Aur Geeta* as the brave fighting hero. An essentially do-gooder, Dharmendra helped Amitabh to get a role in *Sholay* and ever after that mythical block buster pair would set the screen on fire. They worked together in Hrishikesh Mukherjee's film, *Chupke Chupke* and later in *Ram Balaram*. Dharmendra was a fighter who purely fought with brawn; Amitabh composed his action with strategy and planning. When cast against Dharmendra, Amitabh appeared clever, a thinker, a planner, and a strategist, and all of which created his action which was not merely the choreographed physical activity of fighting stunts and body doubles on sets.

Shatrughan Sinha

Shatrughan Sinha is the tough guy who was a superstar in Dulal Guha's *Kalicharan* in 1976. His image is of an action hero who uses his physical power to conceal a deeply sentimental heart. His brawn hides a soft mind; he is quick to get hurt and is emotionally vulnerable. Shatrughan hides his emotions, Amitabh suppresses them, and together, they emerge a sentimental pair on screen and exhaust passions which often make the heroine quite unnecessary. Their film together, *Dostana*, is a high emotion drama; swelling sentiments and welling tears make this movie a memorable work in the genre of friendship movies.

Amjad Khan

Amjad Khan has been the all-time super villain, commanding an equal position as the bad guy as Amitabh Bachchan did in the realm of the heroes. Amjad and Amitabh had been friends for quite a while and their eventual falling apart was not before they made some really outstanding movies together. They were together in *Sholay, Satte Pe Satta, Muqaddar ka Sikandar* and in *Yarana*, last of which was Amjad's role as a co-hero to Amitabh and not a villain. Amjad was an actor who had his own space irrespective of whether Amitabh played against him or not but when Amitabh did act opposite Amjad in the latter's role as the villain, the hero could expand limitlessly. Amjad's badness was limitless, his villainy boundless and Amitabh had the widest scope in straddling the world seeking the villain, in order to demolish him.

Rajesh Khanna

It will not be fair to consider Rajesh Khanna as Amitabh's co-star, for Amitabh was a supporting star for Rajesh Khanna. Rajesh Khanna was a fantasy, a desire, one who was everyone's imagination, while Amitabh is grounded, and is found in well-defined contexts, in specific and even in institutionalised spaces. Amitabh can only stay back while Rajesh Khanna literally flies off; a star partnership with Rajesh Khanna would have forever stalled Amitabh in his journey to stardom. Starring with Amitabh as the supporting role may have taken Rajesh Khanna to higher levels but for Rajesh to flourish, Amitabh would have to be kept indoors. Vinod Khanna, much like Rajesh Khanna, would have undermined Amitabh's prospects, because he would draw out the outer limit within which Amitabh could work.

Rishi Kapoor and Mithun Chakravarty

Two stars who withstood Amitabh's tide were Rishi Kapoor and Mithun Chakravarty. Rishi Kapoor was an overnight star with the release of *Bobby* in 1973, also the year when *Zanjeer* was released. Bobby was about teenage romance and love between a rich boy and a poor girl and Rishi's popularity soared to overtake Rajesh Khanna's for that moment. Assuming that he has arrived on the anvil of superstardom and almost sure that he had beaten Rajesh Khanna to the slot, Rishi was rudely shocked when he realised that not the ruling romantic hero, but the dark horse angry young man in the form of Amitabh Bachchan stood in his way. As if to avenge Rishi Kapoor's rise, Rajesh Khanna married Dimple Kapadia and Rishi though not romantically involved with her, nonetheless faced the loss of his lead heroine. With his co-star gone out of the circuit and romance driven out of the frames with Amitabh's rise, Rishi 'swam against the tide'.[1] But it is to his credit that he filled in the much needed romantic slot in Amitabh's movies and helped the viewer breathe a little easy under the heavy weather of Amitabh's ideologies. In his autobiography, Rishi Kapoor writes that it was he who became indispensable in *Amar Akbar Anthony* and *Kabhie Kabhie* and even in *Naseeb* as Amitabh's co-star, and it was as if Amitabh could never have played the roles he did without Rishi supporting him.[2] Rishi was pure, simple, young, and spontaneous and in love, something that Amitabh's image could never reach out to, and hence, Rishi Kapoor was called again and again to fill in this huge lack in Amitabh's films.

The other superstar who ran parallel to Amitabh in popularity and box office success was Mithun Chakravarty. In the heydays of Amitabh Bachchan, it was said that the actor ranked from the first to the tenth position but the star who ranked the eleventh was Mithun Chakravarty. Mithun had his own territory and is one of the most exported star after Raj Kapoor, especially to Eurasia and Russia. Interestingly, Mithun debuted in Mrinal Sen's film, *Mrigaya*, a director who Amitabh always yearned to work for. Amitabh did a voice over for Sen's film, *Bhuvan Shome*. Mithun was an action hero much like Amitabh Bachchan but he had his own niche; parallel to Amitabh Bachchan, there were some territories especially in the tier 2 cities where cine-goers recognised only Mithun Chakravarty, so much so that when for *Ganga Jamuna Saraswati*, Manmohan Desai reached out to wider audiences, Mithun was the obvious choice. Amitabh's personal

---

1 Rishi Kapoor's autobiography is a good source of information. See Rishi Kapoor. Khullam Khulla. Harper Collins. Delhi. 2017.

2 ibid. and https://www.youtube.com/watch?v=qBAw1Z02mz8

behaviour with Mithun used to be cold and stand-offish and often rather vicious.[3]

Often playing the role of an orphan in his movies, Mithun's image was not one who accumulated anger and collected weapons against villains like Amitabh did, but of one who collected good will, and good guidance along the way to achieve his ends, defeating villains if they stood in the way. Mithun's projects were soulful and spiritual, generous and reaching out and he remained a man who could be closer to you rather than the great distance and height from which Amitabh reigned. Mithun struggled with his own fate rather than desire to change systems; this is why, though a Naxalite revolutionary in his personal life, Mithun did not play a revolutionary on screen. He was too poor and hapless in his screen characters to think of systems and institutions; he had to fight to stay alive than have the surplus to pontificate on the deeper malaise of the world.

3 Soumya Bandopadhyay. Amitabh Bachchan. Bengali. Ananda Publishers. Kolkata. 1995. Pp 148-149.

With Women

The Female Gaze in Indian Popular Cinema

Contrary to Laura Mulvey's thesis that popular arts like cinema, television and advertisement is a male gaze, the popular arts in India has surprisingly been a female gaze.[1] The histories of the United States of America and that of India are different and distinct and these differences create the differences in the predominant gaze. The story of new India lies in a kind of an individual liberation, and somehow a mark of that liberation came to rest on a certain way that womanhood was constituted in the society. Idealistically, women were supposed to enjoy greater sexual freedom in being freed from child marriage, allowed remarriage on the event of widowhood, legally were free to choose their spouse and were supposed to be educated as well as any male member of her family. These freedoms in the newly-framed Constitution at the time of Independence, conceptualised for women, corresponded with the overall framework of individual freedom in which a man could marry of his own choice, pursue a career of his choice, earn for himself and keep the money for his consumption and set up his own home, in which his wife, the homemaker, would be the lone mistress. The woman who would

1 Laura Mulvey. "Visual Pleasure and Narrative Cinema" Screen 16, no. 4 (1975): 6-18.

therefore be the wife of this modern man would have to have modern sensibilities, be fashionable and presentable in the public space, and more or less in all cases found to inhabit the public space only. Heroes would meet their heroines in public spaces like in parks, in hotels, college, travelling by train or by road, and even sometimes in bars and brothels. Only those men were heroes who appealed to women; and indeed heroes of the popular Hindi cinema followed the Indian tradition of the 'ramanimohan' or 'ramaniraman' or 'radharaman', all names of Lord Krishna to depict his desirability among women. This made the feminine gaze a constituting factor of the popular Hindi movie.

Amitabh's Masculinity is Not Brawn

Amitabh Bachchan is said to have brought in a regime of masculinity in the movies. His fights, the exhibition of his body contours, his aloofness to sexual intimacy, lack of romance and sentiments which he had but would repress and crush, took away from the image the softness that the Hindi film heroes were expected to have. Yet, Amitabh was not about brawn; his strong rationality, articulate logic and reasoned arguments made him a man whose masculinity was in his mind. There was another aspect to Amitabh's masculinity and which to my mind is very important. Sunil Dutt was brawny and bucolic and had a pastoral kind of masculinity that appealed to women even when he was rough with them, but in the frames of the films in which he acted, the women's interest, or the foregrounding of her well-being, was never compromised; films still remained about his heroines to whom Sunil Dutt was the hero. In Amitabh's film, he was a hero to himself and never lived to please a woman. Romance was at best a reluctant routine even when he lived the life of an unrequited lover in *Kabhie Kabhie*. The fulcrum of the cinema had changed towards the masculine interest. This is sociologically a very important development and Amitabh Bachchan was that development. An essay elsewhere in this volume addresses the issue of masculinity in greater detail.

Irrelevance of Women in Amitabh's Films

A possible reason why the woman became irrelevant in Amitabh's movies is because her vulnerability which revolved around her body came to inhere the hero's body. It is the hero who is the subject of violence and of violation; he is beaten up, tattooed, made to witness the murder of his parents, and made to suffer the indignity of poverty and even confinement or incarceration. His body now becomes the site of social dangers, something that would usually be the case with the heroine. The dangers were no longer only sexual, they were now social, economic and political.

The films of Amitabh represented a different experience of the Indian society from the time when the modernising individual would come in as the beacon of liberal values to the tradition-bound domestic spaces into the present times, when the family needed to move out of familiar social structures to earn a livelihood and that too most probably in the city. Industrialisation that made cities grow in post-Independence India and created the need for people to be better educated, better clothed, and better groomed in order to be able to participate in an industrialising world, especially for upward social mobility. Clearly then families that wanted to move up the social ladder and concentrate resources to equip children, would have preferred the male child over the female. Indeed, as opportunities for education and employment increased, the need to invest in a child also increased and gender discrimination grew too; female foeticide and infanticide became disturbing trends. The reflection of the gender divide, in which the male child was nudged ahead while the female was kept back to reduce the number of competitors, emerged in the form of Amitabh Bachchan taking up the feminine issues of bodily security in his films. The heroines were then constructed to suit male gaze, if not male perverted gaze. Zeenat Aman and Parveen Babi were heroines to have been used mainly as performers in Amitabh starrers.

Rekha

Rekha withstood the compromise in her dignity by asserting a kind of pastorality. She was a moral force in *Khoon Pasina*, *Ganga ki Saugandh* and *Mr Natwarlal*, *Suhaag* and in *Muqaddar Ka Sikandar*. She bore the image of the eternally suffering woman in love and one who dies for her unrequited love, raised her to a position of reckon. Rekha positioned herself as Amitabh's lady love in real life and perhaps this was a way in which she escaped from being rendered into a wall flower. She has the sizzling erotic appeal which could dissolve the asceticism of Amitabh. People have never been tired of imagining them together and Yash Chopra's film, *Silsila* cast Rekha as the 'other woman' against Jaya who acted as Amitabh's wife in the film. Rekha exuded the power to seduce a man away from his wife, and yet, as a woman in love, refused to exert this power over her lover. She was inwardly autonomous and independent, powerful and commanding, and yet, in love she chooses to remain subservient, only to please her man. Rekha was the only heroine who Amitabh could never wholly consume.

Rakhi

Rakhi was urbane; suave and sophisticated. Rakhi was always seen at a distance with the hero; pretty, dispassionate and aloof. It seemed that Amitabh and Rakhi avoided each other on screen; Rakhi was emerging as a superstar with her double role in *Sharmilee* and her role in *Daag*, and was for some time slated to replace Sharmila Tagore as the poor man's Sharmila, especially as the former took far too many breaks due to her repeated pregnancies. But unfortunately, for her, Amitabh's coup totally changed the Hindi film into a male affair and her career bore the brunt of it. Interestingly, Rakhi has never spoken about Amitabh Bachchan in any interview or reminiscences except with detachment.

Sharmila Tagore

There were a few films that Amitabh acted opposite Sharmila Tagore; a powerful actress, who called shots on sets, rose to superstardom opposite Shammi Kapoor and Rajesh Khanna. Shammi was the entertainer and she the entertained; Rajesh Khanna was the dream and she was the dreamer and it was she, who through her sufferings invoked the image of the hero as a sublime liberator. In a way, the image of the hero was her imagination, born out of her struggles, and in her desire to overcome those struggles. Amitabh's image was that of an embattled man himself; he lived through the pain, worked towards overcoming it; he neither dreamt nor could be a dream for a woman. Sharmila Tagore and Amitabh could never have paired well, for they represented very different forces.

Nutan

Nutan was a towering figure of the cinema when she acted opposite Amitabh in *Saudagar*. Nutan is a woman who lives in confinement; contrary to the usual site of the open public spaces for the heroine, Nutan is found indoors. In *Bandini* she is the prisoner, in *Sujata* she is a Cinderella-like character, and in *Paying Guest* in which she is the landlady, she is held in confinement by her circumstances. To my mind, Amitabh's image too is one who is trapped and who rises to free himself. He is found in confinement; trapped in poverty and confined to lead the life of drudgery as a coolie, or as a police officer or in exile. Rarely, if at all, Amitabh straddles the natural landscape and no wonder when he travels across the sea in *Agneepath*, it becomes such a moment of exhilaration. Nutan remains confined but her montage is spacious; Amitabh's frames always close in while hers always look towards the boundless exterior, and this difference in the organisation of spaces in the montage makes it difficult to hold the two actors in the same frame.

Hema Malini

Hema Malini, again a superstar in the making, who set the screens on fire against Dharmendra, seems slighted in Amitabh's movies, with little left for her to do. Hema Malini, the heroine of *Seeta Aur Geeta*, became the feisty Basanti of *Sholay*, but thereafter cast opposite Amitabh Bachchan in *Satte Pe Satta* or *Desh Premee*, she had little agency left in her except to shadow him. Hema Malini continued to act in films like *Razia Sultan* and *Meerabai*, in which she was the lead star. Her sterling performance in *Andha Kanoon* was not opposite Amitabh Bachchan. In *Trishul* and *Do Aur Do Paanch* she was cast opposite Shashi Kapoor and not Amitabh Bachchan. Hema Malini seemed to have ducked the trend of the male hero and held on to her female-centred films and in this, she seems to be the only heroine left in the industry after the avalanche of Amitabh Bachchan. This may have made Amitabh envious of her for he behaved coldly towards her. Only recently in *Baghban* when the actors played an elderly couple, does Hema Malini shine in her elements again opposite Amitabh, but only when age has substantially mellowed him.

Remakes

In the genre of popular culture, films are often remade scene by scene or with some modifications. Amitabh's film, *Deewar*, was a clear reinterpretation of *Mother India*, a blockbuster that Mehboob Khan made some two decades previously as well as *Ganga Jumna*, a film Bimal Roy made a decade earlier to *Deewar*. *Laawaris*, yet again an Amitabh starrer, had shades of Raj Kapoor's *Awara*. Similarly, some of Amitabh's films have been remade as well, like *Zanjeer, Agneepath* and *Don*. Shah Rukh Khan, the reigning superstar of India, one who many imagined would replace Amitabh Bachchan as the megastar, played the role of Don in the movie named after its lead character. *Chaalbaaz* of 1989 is the director Pankaj Parashar's frame to frame remake of the classic *Seeta Aur Geeta* in 1973, directed by Ramesh Sippy. *Chaalbaaz* was Sridevi's portrayal of Hema Malini's role in the earlier film.

Remakes challenge the older films in an act of defiance when the new aspirants want a straight fight with the older stars. The remake is a rewriting, a generational warfare, attempts at dislodging the older classic from the memory and etching a new story in the minds of people. Remakes are vandalisms. Often presented in the garb of a tribute, remakes are attempts at displacing older works from the mind maps of viewers and overwriting, with no other purpose except to boast and defy the respectability of the yore. Remakers conceal under the garb of tribute payers, with the most despicable desire to obliterate and wreck classic productions.

This section discusses primarily the remake of *Deewar*, *Don* and *Agneepath* because the essays contained in this volume are only illustrative and not exhaustive and intends only to raise some points rather than encyclopaedically cover the entire gamut of films which have been remade, perhaps several times over the years.

Amitabh's film, *Deewar,* was a clear reinterpretation of *Mother India*, a blockbuster that Mehboob Khan made some two decades previously as well as *Ganga Jumna*, a film Bimal Roy made a decade earlier to *Deewar*. *Deewar* conversed with both predecessors, articulated issues of its own by reworking many aspects of the earlier films to make a more rebellious discourse of its own. *Laawaris*, yet again an Amitabh starrer, had shades of Raj Kapoor's *Awara*. Similarly, some of Amitabh's films have been remade as well, like *Zanjeer*, *Agneepath* and *Don*. Shah Rukh Khan, the reigning superstar of India, one who many imagined would replace Amitabh Bachchan as the megastar, played the role of Don in the movie named after its lead character.

Don and Don

Don made in 1978 was written by Salim and Javed and Chandra Barot, a man of few directorial ventures, directed the film. Except for the story, *Don* borrowed heavily in terms of rhythm, background score and montage frames and flavours from *Agent Vinod*, a thriller that was made a year before. *Agent Vinod* was a pure thriller with a kidnapped scientist, an investigator and his love interest who is the daughter of the kidnapped man. *Don* had a kidnapped police officer, a police agent, a girl whose brother was killed by Don, the dreaded criminal. There was a cabaret dancer, a den of baddies, disguise, climbing up and down high rise apartment buildings by long ropes and most shots were at night. But there the similarities end. The purpose of *Don* was to use the format of *Agent Vinod* in order to hang the real tale, a tale that was a series of impersonations.

A relative new comer, Mahendra Sandhu played the role of Vinod, while Amitabh Bachchan, already a superstar, acted in the role of Don. Films that are made with relative newcomers may belong to the directors or the actors but films that have superstars in them are scripted with a purpose of exploring the image of the star. There may indeed be many exceptions, but on the whole, this habit of deciding the auteur of the film seems to be the rule. Don is a ruthless man who is wanted by the police of 11 countries and who evades the police in ingenious ways. He kills with abandon and executes his aides on the slightest hint of evidence that they may be agents of the police. Despite his invincibility, Don is killed in a police encounter. The police, using the belief among the people that Don is invincible, places a look alike, the street singer called Vijay, as Don.

The crux of Don is the chase; unlike *Agent Vinod* in which the hero chases the villain, in Don, Amitabh as the character in a double role chases himself. Don is smart and suave, devastatingly attractive and lethally effectual, while Vijay is street smart and is a man of small means, crude and unfashionable and even uneducated. He is a street singer, the kind of man who often in Hindi films becomes a police informer and in popular mind becomes a petty thief. The chase set to a background staccato gels well as an action movie, but the chase of Don is not of the hero and the villain as much as it is Vijay chasing the absent image of Don and becoming like him. At one level, Vijay is seen ducking Don's men, while on the other hand, he pretends to be running away from the police; he runs away quite a bit from the heroine who thinks Vijay to be Don and wants to kill him; and at yet another level, Vijay runs to literally catch up with Don who seems to be far ahead in sophistication, intellect and wealth. The last aspect of Don is engaging, for this is the crux of Amitabh Bachchan's image; always evolving, always learning, transforming and transmuting, metamorphosing and resurrecting.

Shah Rukh Khan also acted in a later version of *Don*, a film that Farhan Akhtar made. *Don's* original script was written by Salim and Javed and *Don*, like *Zanjeer*, *Deewar* and *Sholay* was a film that defined Amitabh Bachchan's persona. *Don* exemplified Amitabh's screen character, the one who always chases an ever-enlarging ideal, an ever-expanding scale. In his real life, Amitabh has always evolved and grown through complete changeovers and makeovers. Don and Amitabh are thus not very different people. Behind Vijay lies the image of Don; cruel, unscrupulous, selfish and power hungry, and interestingly, Amitabh Bachchan, whether in his affair with Rekha, scandals of Bofors and Panama and accusations from Parveen Babi of him trying to kill her, emerges as a philander, schemer and a planner, who uses everybody for his own selfish end.

Farhan Akhtar, the director and writer of the remake of *Don*, watched the original version of the film when he was only 11-years old. Smitten by the film, he decided to remake it as he thought it would intensify the pleasure for the audience. The frames of the film have been made as if to return to the audience the pleasure of watching the original.

A film has two aspects; one that is shown and the one which is felt, absorbed and ruminated upon. Farhan's film was made by absorbing the viewer's surplus into the film in a way of absorbing both, the grain and the chaff, and this is why there was so little that came out of the film by way of adding to the persona of Shah Rukh Khan. Were *Don* never to be made, Shah Rukh would lose nothing, but were *Don* never to be made; Amitabh may never have attained the star persona that he has. The background score of the new *Don* had similar notes but a more mechanical and stretched beat. The rhythm of the music of the original *Don* that was similar to *Agent Vinod* of 1977, helped to discover the innate body movement of Amitabh Bachchan, and thus, seemed to set the pace and pitch of his films. In case of the remake, the music had to be reworked to suit the rhythm of Shah Rukh Khan's body, and because the movements of Shah Rukh and Amitabh are very different, *Don's* rhythm in case of Shah Rukh Khan had practically no function, because the beat was set to Amitabh's body movements.

Amitabh is very earthy and bodily, for it is upon this body that he takes the beating, the torture, the strain. Shah Rukh forces his way in the world through his obsessive mind which he uses as a weapon to hit his target continuously until the walls of resistance break down. Shah Rukh's fights are jerky and random; they are not directed at effecting change or transforming the underlying conditions of existence. He breaks through people's resistances through his obsessiveness. Don, as portrayed by Shah Rukh, is therefore an obsessive character, and which is out of character with Amitabh's Don. Shah Rukh becomes dangerous as he raises his obsessions into insane levels; Amitabh's lethality and power stems from the fact that he never loses his mind to obsessions, can control his passions and reign in emotions.

Amitabh's is not an obsessive mind; his is a mind that is free of emotional attachments, except when emotions concern the protection of the weak like a mother or a child, or the poor. Don is not the 'complete' Amitabh; he is completed by Vijay who does the risky impersonation. Don is heartless while Vijay is soulful. He had no business to take the orphans under his wings but he did that, even without asking who they were. The protective element of Vijay fits in with the lethality of Don, and together, they create a single image of Amitabh, the superstar. The film Don, not only discovers Amitabh's rhythm, but it creates the image of the star as one who brings together the various and often conflicting images of characters played on screen.

In the version of Shah Rukh Khan, Don survives Vijay; it is Don who kills Vijay rather than in Amitabh's version where Vijay catches up with Don. The original film's hero is the dead Don and Vijay chases the image, and as he progressively becomes Don, it appears that he resurrects the character. Vijay's target is to become Don and through his chase of the image, creates among the viewers, a desire to see Don again. Farhan Akhtar's version plays on the audience's fantasies that Don could've been alive and Vijay could be the real Don who was all the while impersonating as Vijay. In Shah Rukh Khan's version, Don does not die, he is the one who lives on even if that means killing on a grand scale. Romi, the sister of the man who Don murdered in Amitabh's version marries Vijay, the good man, while in Shah Rukh's version, she marries Don, smitten by the bad man's charms. Don can charm anyone, which includes winning the heart of a lady who has come to kill him. Farhan Akhtar who works on the film on the memories of an 11-year old seems to have looked at the film with a child's eye and hence, may have missed the importance of the music and the discovery of the body movement of the star; Amitabh Bachchan in this case.

The different versions of *Don* reveal the differences between Amitabh and Shah Rukh Khan. Shah Rukh resists death and by refusing to allow Don to die, he shows him to be acquisitive, one who wants to add on to the image and refuses to let go. Amitabh, on the other hand, is a man of death; he dies, revives, reincarnates and reinvents himself many times. This attribute makes the image of Amitabh capable of absorbing and fitting in a variety of attributes, creating spaces for many directors to work with him; Shah Rukh, despite his huge fan following, remains a man of a coterie, one who only a few can use and make use of. Despite Prakash Mehra, Manmohan Desai, Yash Chopra and the late Mukul Anand, Amitabh has worked extensively with various directors, even in their one off films with him.

Amitabh's dissolution is his nihilism and this nihilism is his appeal; life and death are not distinct for Amitabh and death cannot annihilate him. No wonder he continues as a star, even when he is 75! Shah Rukh is essentially the lover, a man of life, and a man who death annihilates and no wonder Shah Rukh cannot let go of his image as easily as Amitabh does, and this makes him adopt shades of a lover even as the elderly psychiatrist in *Dear Zindagi*.

Agneepath and Agneepath

Shakespeare has influenced Indian theatre and cinema to an observable extent. Shakespeare's Romeo and Juliet has been adapted endlessly into Hindi films and Vishal Bhardwaj in contemporary times has adapted many of Shakespeare's tragedies such as Macbeth, Hamlet and Othello into films. Mukul Anand's *Agneepath* made in 1990 seems to be the adaptation of Julius Caesar, in which Amitabh, called Vijay, plays the role of Caesar. The film starts with the assassination of Caesar when Vijay's competitors from his own gang gun him down on the sea beach. Vijay miraculously survives as a wayside coconut seller, a role played by Mithun Chakravarty, takes him to the hospital and gets him treated. In the rest of the film, Vijay plays a ghost-like character, as if Caesar's ghost has appeared to avenge his own death. The ghost-like image did very well for Amitabh, yet, the box office shunned the film and the losses were substantial according to Karan Johar's accounts[1]. Amitabh spoke through the film in a cracked voice like a ghost but the viewers did not accept the alteration to the star's signature baritone and the film had to be released in Amitabh's usual tone. *Agneepath* became Amitabh's post mortem portrayal of Vijay.

---

1 Poonam Saxena. Karan Johar - An Unsuitable Boy. Penguin India. 2017. Pg 31.

Agneepath was remade in 2012 with Hrithik Roshan in the lead as Vijay. The choice of Hrithik is interesting because he is not one of the reigning Khans, nor is he a quintessential Shakespearean character like Saif or Ajay Devgan or even Shaheed Kapoor. But his image has an enormous power of resurrection. Hrithik's debut film, *Kaho Na Pyar Hai* and which made him into a superstar at once, projects the star in a double role in which he is dead and is then reborn. *Kaho Na*... is not a story of a rebirth, for rebirth films are those in which the hero refuses to die. It will not be out of the context to mention that Shah Rukh Khan, Rishi Kapoor and even the mighty Rajesh Khanna and Dilip Kumar have done films of rebirth, while Amitabh has never played such a role. Sometimes, like in *Don* or *Kasme Vaade*, Amitabh has died as one character and returned as someone very different, but has never been reborn or resurrected. Amitabh's is an ongoing journey of an ever-evolving being; one who transforms every moment to emerge into ever newer selves. For such a person, life and death becomes woven into one another, rendering rebirths redundant.

Hrithik's is an image for which resurrection is possible; much like Rajesh Khanna in *Aradhana*, where he reappears, or returns to Sharmila Tagore. The two characters of Rohit and Raj, both played by Hrithik, are disconnected, giving us a sense, not of rebirth, but of death in which bodies and memories are all obliterated, a rational death, a believable death. To my mind, this post-death quality of Hrithik's image was perhaps a reason why he was chosen for the remake of *Agneepath*.

In *Agneepath*, Hrithik suffered. In *Agneepath*, Amitabh had already moved beyond suffering, and in fact, his wife had to remind him of the revenge he promised on Kancha Cheena. The quality of *Agneepath* was a resurrection for Amitabh, one for who both anger and suffering, action and revenge were exhausted, and one who looked tired and done with through the film. The hero had to be nudged to take action and provoked deeply, as he lay dying in his mother's lap, much like the death scene in *Deewar*, though he showed none of the softness that came upon him in *Deewar*. The hero returned home to his mother in *Deewar*; in *Agneepath*, the hero returned to his mother to clarify some of her mistaken notions, before he finally left his purgatory.

Amitabh's image in *Agneepath* came with the exhaustion of nearly every possibility with that image. For Hrithik, the role in *Agneepath* came a bit too early, when the image had not gone through as many shades as Amitabh's had done. Besides, Hrithik has precisely no image which he stands for; he has no back up theory; his body has a strangely magical flavour as he appears and disappears in *Kaho Na Pyar Hai*, in *Fiza*, *Koi Mil Gaya* and even in *Krishh*. Amitabh's is a grounded body, it suffers bodily pain, can inflict bodily pain on others as well; the body is a site of experiences and is a site for making sense of those experiences. This is why, Amitabh could play a role in which he is shot at by his comrades many times and in several angles, just as Caesar was stabbed by his cohorts repeatedly. If Amitabh had not carried the image of Caesar within him, he could never have played the role in *Agneepath*. On the other hand, Hrithik is not a Caesar, and hence, his role did not do too well. Hrithik's career graph has not done too well in the Hindi film industry, especially when we consider that he started off with an enormous promise in his debut film; a possible reason for this could be that his is an image which can absorb very little.

The magic of *Agneepath* was the ghost-like movement of Amitabh, interrupted by moments of intense emergence of the body. Blood and gore, sweat and tears created the bodily feelings when most of the times the hero moved as if he was in the purgatory, burning in Hell. *Agneepath* created a massive visual of the hero and his gang, chasing through the narrow alleys of the slum, a scene which alone may have inspired the recently released Bengali film, *Zulfikar* by Shrijeet Mukherjee, based on Shakespeare's Julius Caesar. The full bodiness of the hero, the near animal-like movement when he emerges against the rising sun in the horizon, and the violent death that he meets, are all placed for the viewer to get the feeling of the body, in order to be compensated for the formlessness of the hero. I think that

Hrithik, with his perfect body, had difficulty in alternating between the ghost-like appearances and then also as a helpless mortal.

One of the magical moments of *Agneepath* by Mukul Anand is Amitabh's journey across the oceans to meet Kancha Cheena. This has the effect of Caesar crossing the seas; and in the film, the scene of the hero moving across the oceans was elating only because Amitabh conveyed a sense of having exhausted his enemies on land. Hrithik's image can barely convey exhaustion of possibilities and hence exhaustion of engagement cannot belong to Hrithik, though the exhaustion of exercise may.

Being Julius Caesar, Deewar and Agneepath

In 2016, Shrijit Mukherjee made *Zulfikar*, a Bengali adaptation of Julius Caesar. The film unfortunately could neither bring out the nuances of Julius Caesar and those of his cohorts involved in the conspiracy to murder the Roman dictator nor could he access Shakespeare in his entire splendor. The film flopped badly despite the heavy-weight star cast and intense publicity. However, the movie brings me to the adaptation of Julius Caesar played by Amitabh Bachchan; the film I speak of is *Agneepath*. *Agneepath* had the same motif of the hero Vijay emerging as more intelligent and capable than his gang, whereby the gang decides to assassinate him. Vijay knows of the plot, yet he goes over steadily to face his death. The spirit of Calpurnia is part in the hero's mother and partly in the police officer, Gaitonde, while Enobarbus is played by Mithun Chakravarty in his character as Shankar Iyer. Tinnu Anand plays the role of a madman but is actually the soothsayer who foresees things. The character Laila played by Archana Puran Singh resembles Cleopatra, who is an aide of the hero but not his romantic interest in the film. Vijay crosses the sea like Caesar to capture his long standing enemy, Kancha Cheena, a role played by Danny Denzongpa. Vijay survives an assassination early on in the film but moves through the rest of the film in a ghost-like form, barely relating to the world of flesh and blood. The blood and gore, the wounds on the hero's body are intense, for these will only give us a sense of his body, for he walks in a state of bodilessness, as if in a dream.

The story of *Agneepath* is not unlike that of *Deewar* in which a boy from a respectable family is forced to take to the streets in order to avenge the murder of his idealist father. He avenges his dead father's humiliation because a mob was set upon the school teacher based on a fake sex scandal. In *Deewar*, his father is also subject to a mob attack after he is set up by the employers on a false case of betrayal. In *Agneepath*, the little boy had to drag his father's body for cremation beyond the limits of the village because of the stigma attached to his father's character. The boy finds no justice with the police and hence decides to join the villains in order to reach Kancha Cheena, the man who was behind it all. The story however is a mere peg to hang the real tale of the hero on, a man who can bring together the ends of the earth, rise from destitution into a position of command, from defenselessness to unbridled dominance, and one who can wait to acquire every resource and then pull out his enemy from whichever corner of the earth he may hide. The hero straddles the social space as well as the geographical space, and all through this, he journeys essentially through time, keeping alive memories, emotions and feelings of humiliation, in order to overcome them. Gaitonde and his mother fear that the thoughts of revenge may harm Vijay, but he is in no mood to relent; in fact, it is the theme of revenge that raises him to the levels of a Caesar that also provokes his assassination. The hero keeps repeating his name as Vijay Dinanath Chauhan by adding the signature phrase, *poora naam*, or complete name signifying, that he carries his dead father with him in his heart. Unlike in *Deewar* in which the hero represses the memories of his father, in *Agneepath*, the hero keeps the father alive, almost like Hamlet's ghost.

Agneepath has been remade with Hrithik Roshan as Vijay who appears more like Augustus Caesar, the nephew of the great Caesar flung into greatness by the dint of legacy. Hrithik Roshan is an accomplished actor and a great star but there is a difference between Amitabh and he; Hrithik's face does not seem to carry memories, his is not a body that carries the past. Amitabh's does. In Soumya Bandopadhya's accounts of Amitabh's biography, he traces his ancestry across seven generations in which a man named Mansa was forced to leave his village during the drought and relocate around Pratapgarh near Allahabad, and the forefathers of Amitabh have lived there ever since. The story of Mansa was recreated in the Amitabh starrer *Adalat*. Amitabh bought a bungalow in Juhu close to his existing one. He named his new home as Mansa. However, under the advice of a numerologist, the name has been changed to Jalsa, but in naming it Mansa, I sense memory in the man. Amitabh is a person of long remembrances. The face shows it – the face that holds long reminiscences.

When *Agneepath* was first released, fans were disappointed with the hoarse voice in which Amitabh spoke in the film, and also, it appeared to be a remake of *Deewar*. The film prints were withdrawn and fresh ones were issued where Amitabh redubbed the film with his original baritone. But the similarities with *Deewar* were disturbing. *Deewar* was a complete film; it was beyond improvisation and fans clearly did not wish to see a looser version of the same film. True there were similarities in the death of the father, in the differences between the mother and the son, and eventually in the death of the hero in his mother's lap in a moment of reconciliation. But there the similarities end. In fact, I think that the similarities were put on purpose to tie up *Agneepath* to *Deewar*, perhaps to throw a hint to the audiences that the film was an end of a journey for Amitabh Bachchan. We may recall that *Agneepath* was made during one of Amitabh's darkest hours when he had tendered in his resignation from politics and was being harassed with bribery charges in the Bofors deal. *Agneepath* was a kind of an emotional return to *Deewar*, the taking of a full circle; as if in a manner of rounding things off before signing out of the industry. The similarities between the two above mentioned films were deliberate and were meant to show the society's disregard and desertion of the once popular hero.

Vijay of *Deewar* was a rising star; his identity was formed in the course of the film's story. Vijay of *Agneepath* is a born hero, aware of his role in the world as in the rainy days he would wipe down the moisture from the window of Kancha's car only to have a close look at the man who ruined him, resolving to turn the tables on him one day. The hero of *Deewar* is an entity who rises from a non-entity, almost invisible as the shoe shine boy. The hero of *Agneepath* is visible even as a child, for he burns down a petrol station which belongs to the villain but eventually becomes invisible. He falls to the bullets of the assassins, rises to murder them one by one and then assumes headship of his gang and eventually crosses the seas to get at Kancha Cheena.

The dark blue colour of the shirt of the hero of *Deewar* now becomes the principle hue of the frames, albeit in a lighter shade. *Agneepath* is shot in shades of blue, the sky, the sea, the ocean, the rain, the shutters and the shades on the roofs of homes. *Agneepath* is spilt out *Deewar*, awash in the waves from the sea. The hero lives in a fragmented world, the montage of *Agneepath* is untidy, bare, bereft and empty unlike the tidy spaces of *Deewar*. *Agneepath* is a world deserted, *Deewar* is a world lived in. *Agneepath* is civil war in the aftermath of Caesar's assassination, while *Deewar* is a world conquered and won by an emerging hero. *Deewar's* hero is celebrated, *Agneepath's* hero is castigated. *Agneepath* uses *Deewar*, both as memory as well as loss. It is that Vijay who was once carried on shoulders of men now must be carried in a coconut cart by the lone Shankar Iyer, in a way not unlike the time when the little boy had carried the corpse of his father. *Agneepath* is the film of emptiness, representing the end of time. Mukul Anand, the director of *Agneepath*, also made *Hum* and *Khuda Gawa*, both about heroes living a life beyond their own time, in a place elsewhere, among different people and unknown communities. None of these films have the groundedness of *Deewar* or *Trishul*, or even of *Kala Paththar*, the films that raised Amitabh to the level of the star that he eventually was to be. Mukul Anand's films were films of the hero past his prime, the hero now out of his active life, beyond the era that held him, past the times that made him.

Awara and Deewar

Amitabh Bachchan is a star because of the way he engages and rises up against a recalcitrant world to establish himself in a normal life in which he can look after his mother, marry and raise his children. So are all the other stars. But the stars of the Hindi film world fight to remove the obstacles in order to reach to the normal life, which the society offers as a worthy goal. Amitabh does not merely remove the obstacles; he fights the very conditions which give rise to the obstacles in the first place. As a hero, Amitabh Bachchan's aim is to eliminate the conditions of the obstacles and only after that, attain the bliss of a normal life as a by-product.

In the image of Amitabh, there appears to be a changeover, from heroes who are passionate romantic into the hero played by Amitabh Bachchan as a reflective, tragic rebel, one who is deeply hurt at being wronged, rises to fight and surpasses himself in abilities which he never knew he possessed. Amitabh's film *Deewar* appears to be in the league of Raj Kapoor's *Awara*, although we do not often think of similarities between the two. Raj Kapoor was not originally supposed to have played the lead role, and though he was to produce the film, the co-collaborator, K.A. Abbas, the writer of the story, wanted Ashok Kumar and Dilip Kumar to play the father and son role, but Raj Kapoor wanted his father, Prithviraj Kapoor to play the father, and him, the son. They parted ways and Raj Kapoor directed the film himself. *Awara* would have been a very different film had Dilip Kumar and Ashok Kumar played the roles, and it is here we may get the idea that a star is not merely a mute conveyor of the script and that the body and the face changes meanings and language.

Awara was the story of a mother and child abandoned by a self-righteous father on the suspicion that the mother was pregnant with the child of a dacoit, Jagga, who kidnapped her. The child grows up to be Raj Kapoor called Raju, while the father is the judge, Justice Raghunath. Raghunath, not too happy with the separation which he brought upon himself raises Rita, played by Nargis, as his own daughter. As Raj fights poverty, Jagga helps him by training him as a thief. But as a thief, his romance with Rita is jeopardised, for there cannot be a transition of this passion into marriage because of the wide differences in social class. The songs, the scenes, the dialogues are more oriented towards romance and the viewer is stressed over whether Raj and Rita can marry at all. The prejudices of Justice Raghunath favouring the purity of birth rather than the merit of nurture are brought in as the major impediments of marriage. Were Dilip Kumar and Ashok Kumar to act in *Awara*, the film would have become emotional and sentimental, with a relationship of father and son under greater importance; but with Raj Kapoor and Prithviraaj Kapoor, the film becomes a contest of ideology, of biases and reason, of institutions and values that hold structures versus values which dissolve them.

Deewar is similar to *Awara* in the sense that here, the father abandons the family, unable to face the problems of life, and the hero as a young boy takes on the responsibilities of the family. The hero of *Deewar* actually has no enemy to fight with but he finds villains in all those spaces which the family encounters while making a livelihood, and these are the men who molest women at work, the extortionists who snatch money away from an honest day's work, the politicians who influence recruitment, the investors who refuse to invest money in gainful businesses, the men who ruin lives and force people into undignified territories, all become the subjects of the hero's anger. There are issues with the absconding father but those remain deep into the recesses of the mind of the hero. The principle focus becomes the hero's fight with the world. Both Amitabh and Raj Kapoor are heavily ideological, but the former is moralistic in his ideology while the latter is ideological in morality.

The two films differ in texture. *Awara* is a set of lightly floating and even fleeting images perhaps to contrast the drab existence of the hero in his world with the sublime beauty of a possible romance which finally redeems him. There is a girl who will take him back to a beautiful world intended for him and from which he has been only temporarily exiled. Poverty is harsh and miserable and in it lurks the temptation of Jagga, but it is an aberration if the hero is Chaplinesque, innocent and besieged. *Deewar* is a series of freeze frames; although extremely fast paced and sharply edited, its frames appear to be pushing brakes, stalling in each moment, as if offended, as if hurt, as if stopped in tracks. *Deewar* is firmly set upon the ground without the relief of sublimity, without hope and into despair. In *Deewar*, poverty is the reality, emancipation is impossible and not even a dream.

The city life makes Raj Kapoor uncomfortable; it is too chaotic and vexing for the hero; on the other hand, Amitabh is born into the city; he is meant to be a part of it, the city braces him and because of his familiarity and ease in the city, he can both see its contradictions and fight them. For Raj Kapoor, the problem lies in characters of humans, while for Amitabh, the problem lies in the nature of opportunities that the city throws up for villainy. When Raj faces a jail sentence and goes behind the bars, he feels a sense of calm at being finally contained in a set of rules; for Amitabh, he is most comfortable in the rules he makes and finds the rules which discipline him to be acontextual, empty, formal and therefore oppressive. Amitabh wants to build institutions but cares little for the existing ones; Raj Kapoor seeks institutions.

The father is the cause of misery in both films; in *Awara*, he actively harms the family, in *Deewar* he merely withdraws from responsibilities, leaving the family to fend for itself. In *Awara*, the hero does not know who the father is but finds him eventually; in *Deewar*, the hero knows his father but never gets to find him except when he is a corpse. The hero in *Awara* does not know his father and rather instinctively chooses Jagga, the criminal, as his mentor and father figure. In *Deewar*, the hero knows his father, constantly accuses him of betrayal and willingly chooses Dawar as a mentor in place of a father. Amitabh Bachchan always knows his enemies and this brings about a direction in his moves, a purpose in his roles, which extends beyond what is merely the montage. If we regard popular culture as something that should travel out of the text into the lives of the people, we may easily infer why Amitabh Bachchan is said to be the star as no star has ever been.

Rita, the lady love in Raj Kapoor's life, waits for him, and carries him away from his misery into prospects of infinite bliss; Anita, the lady love in Amitabh's life in *Deewar* pulls him down into the vortex of 'sin' that will ultimately ruin him. Raj Kapoor gets a fairy tale-like quality through his women on screen; Amitabh is rendered earthier through the women in the narrative. Raj Kapoor's image has a strong sexuality; it is not really masculine but that of an adolescent, who is in the process of discovery of the erotic. Amitabh is matured, in a way wholly matured, absolved either of sexual curiosity or of guilt, risen fairly above sex and engages in it consciously, in full awareness.

In both films, *Awara* and *Deewar,* the mother is a prominent prop for the hero to develop. In both films, she is the one who the hero wants to protect from poverty and misery, and in both films, she is the source of morals for the hero. For the image of Raj Kapoor, she merely teaches him values; in *Deewar*, she actually disciplines him. The mother in Amitabh's films rises as the significant woman, above the heroine, to engage with the hero in many more frames than what the heroine does. The mother is not an adolescent attachment; for Amitabh's roles, her importance travels to the hero's adulthood, even past his youth, when he must raise a family similar to the one he was raised in, or supposed to have been raised in. Amitabh is therefore past romance, past marriage, already in the figure of the father, because even when he is only a young man, as in *Deewar*, all that he thinks is of protecting his family and many families like his in similar state of helplessness that poverty throws them into.

Deewar, Mother India and Ganga Jumna

Deewar, the film that is undoubtedly Amitabh Bachchan's basic text, creating in him a hero that the Hindi filmdom has never seen, is not too original a story and not too ingenious in its dialogues. The outstanding dialogue between Shashi Kapoor and Amitabh Bachchan where each seek their last chance at reconciliation before the commencement of the epic battle is taken straight out from *Mughal-e-Azam*. Besides this, *Deewar* can well be said to be a remake of *Mother India* as well as *Ganga Jumna*, two very different films but punched together in Amitabh's sterling appearance.

Mother India is the story of Radha who takes up the role of the breadwinner after her husband flees home. Her husband can no longer withstand the pain of his disability and disappears from the life of his wife and children. Radha faces sexual harassment, financial ruin, hunger, destitution and humiliation, all of which she overcomes and emerges again as a respectable member of her community. Through her journey, her son Birju rebels many times, unable to tolerate the pain that his mother goes through. Radha reprimands Birju for being intemperate because she believes that absorbing everything stoically is the way to preserve oneself in the world.

In *Deewar*, Birju becomes Vijay, the son, who is unable to see his mother suffering and alights in the streets to make a livelihood so that his mother's burdens are reduced and pain eased. Vijay grows up with the capabilities to amass wealth and power but his mother opposes him by accusing him of having made it out through illegitimate means. In *Mother India*, Radha shoots down Birju for kidnapping the girl he loves; in *Deewar* none of such passions are played out. Vijay is rational and argumentative and he and his mother argue over the idea of what constitutes legitimate behavior.

Law, argues Vijay, cannot be a problem of social order and it has to be an empowering institution to facilitate the meritorious to access opportunities from which they have been deprived. The mother is pushed out as a challenger of the hero in *Deewar*, and the hero, instead of the mother, now takes centre stage.

In *Ganga Jumna*, the older brother Ganga earns to educate his brother Jumna, and the latter becomes a police officer. Ganga, who faces a hard life and is exposed to violence, reacts with violence to defend himself. In this act of using violence against violence, in the eyes of law, Ganga becomes a criminal. Jumna is all set to arrest him. In *Deewar*, Vijay works as a child labourer to send his younger brother Ravi to school, and Ravi, now in his role as a police officer, is all set to arrest Vijay. The dialogues between Ganga and Jumna are sentimental and tear jerking but the crux of the interchanges are similar to those in *Deewar*. It seems that *Deewar* has chaffed out the logic from the emotions, brushed out the sentiments, suppressed the tears hard and emerged wholly into hardened rationality and totally objective intellect. *Deewar's* tears are not apparent on screen, but one feels them while watching the movie, remembering it, and while talking about the film.

Jumna remembers the sacrifices that Ganga made for him in order to pay for his education; Ravi never acknowledges Vijay's contribution towards his life and instead makes Vijay into a villain for attempting to raise the family out of poverty, of which Ravi has been the prime beneficiary. Jumna appears to be genuinely bound by law and pained by his compulsions of having to arrest Ganga, Ravi somewhere appears as if he enjoys nailing in Vijay of who he may have been secretly resentful because his mother loved Vijay more. In his loyalty towards the law, Ravi is inhuman and Jumna helpless. *Ganga Jumna* is a drama, *Deewar* is an execution.

The privilege of the single hero, the repression of the emotions, and the foregrounding of hard logic, make *Deewar* a political film in which the hero argues his case against law, along the principles of jurisprudence, raising ethical questions pertaining to social inequality and distribution of entitlements and legitimacies, which constitute the social structure. The change in focus with which *Deewar* rewrites the stories of the above mentioned films, is with the intent of politicisation of the Hindi popular cinema, and to make popular culture weigh heavy on the politics of its times.

Equality and Anxiety

Observers often say that politics of the times affects the construction of the hero and that Amitabh Bachchan's rebellious demeanour reflected the mood of the nation at the time. The 1970's, say the contemporary historians, were turbulent times, when nearly every kind of organised sector of the economy rose in agitation over the State and its institutions[1]. Mrs Gandhi, the then prime minister, declared the Emergency, suspending every kind of democratic rights and directed the State against the citizens; so say the contemporary observers[2].

Looked at carefully, the strikes and the protests and the anti-establishment politics of the people were somehow tied to the excitability of a new era. Despite the end of Mrs Gandhi's first term in the Emergency of 1975, the era was one of deepening of democracy, for those sections that were hitherto at the margins, were included in the mainstream for the first time. In the times of Mrs Gandhi's prime ministership, which extended from 1966 to 1977 in as many as two stints, the Parliament passed as many as 50 laws that addressed equality.

These new laws included the freeing of bonded labour, development programmes for drought prone areas and hilly

1 Bipan Chandra et al. India Since Independence – 1947-2000. Penguin. Delhi. 2000. Pp 232-233.

2 Emergency was declared on 25th June 1975

terrains, fixing of minimum wages for workers, making dowry demands acts of crime, and spread of education and economic aid for the Dalits, tribals and women.

Public institutions like the IITs, the medical colleges, government hospitals, railways, postal departments, the public sector, public works and the bureaucracy expanded, giving a larger scope to an ever expanding and an increasingly-aspiring middle class, to establish themselves into relative prosperity.

Lefebvre writes of the French Revolution that revolutions are possible only when the prospect of gains are evident and this happens in times of emerging prosperity and not during crushing poverty.[3] The polity promised equality and created fresh aspirations among people to emerge into the middle-class mainstream. The availability of avenues of upward mobility was, in my mind, a more vital cause for political restlessness and civic strife. Amitabh Bachchan's films were born out of this kind of anxious excitement over the opening up of possibilities of improving one's social status. Thrilled by a new confidence, albeit received from the possibilities of growth of public investments, people became more assertive and unruly, perhaps out of the psychology that since they have greater opportunities for rewards, they could stretch the limits of their bargaining. The industrial and institutional unrests which gave scope for politics to intensify were perhaps born more due to the excitement of hopes of gain than out of the despondency of doom. Amitabh's image of the angry young man, forever shaking up the institutions in order to open these up to make way for larger participation, suited the mood of its times. The hero's politics was one of seeking greater equality in opportunity, which only the State could provide, and this matched by the politics of Mrs Gandhi in expanding the State. Amitabh, thus, resonated Indira Gandhi's own fight with the more conservative elements within the Congress, known as the Syndicalists, with whom she broke away to constitute her own party, the Youth Congress, or the Congress Republicans.

3 Georges Lefebvre. The French Revolution – From Its Origins to 1793. Routledge. Taylor and Francis. South Asian Edition. London and New York. 2005.

The cinema before Indira Gandhi and therefore before Amitabh Bachchan was drunk with the excitement of individual freedom, which came with modernity, a product of decolonisation.

It had everything to do with setting forth of ideal individuals within a society which was more or less unified despite its internal stratification. The cinema of Amitabh just as the politics of Indira Gandhi was not about being the ideal but being victorious; here men of the lower classes challenged the upper classes and won against them. Theirs was a divided society where not social consensus but contests and conflict dwelled.

The cinema before Amitabh Bachchan's *Zanjeer* in 1974 could be called romantic cinema, in which individuality over social roles was the principle anxiety of men and women. By the time Amitabh Bachchan came, in the 1970's, the first flush of romanticism had gone through its cycle of maturity, a new age emerged upon India, an age which we may call as the 'age of status anxiety'[4]. Defined as an age of future and of expectations, when people start thinking in terms of a future, they develop expectations from meritocracy rather than from snobbery, and in which they also start looking at the various ways in which they are dependent on the system. De Botton says that on the one hand they bargain with their employers for better wages, while on the other hand, they realize that the enterprise needs to do better in the overall market place. Thus, bargaining is both; improvement in power vis-à-vis the employer, as well as increasing the overall capacity of institutions. Amitabh's films and Indira Gandhi's politics did both.

Amitabh's films centred on anxiety for better social opportunities; for this, institutions needed to expand, power of the talented individual within institutions needed to increase, the society needed to be more facilitative of merit rather than respect the entrenched inequalities. This was an age for demanding equality, only if that equality meant the destruction of the privileges, so that the congealed asymmetries in wealth

---

4 Alain De Botton. Status Anxiety. Penguin. UK. 2004. Pp45-46.

and power could be dissolved to make way for the new. This is Ayn Rand's thesis of equality[5]. De Botton says that such anxiety in the society is often resolved through politics, art, philosophy and religion, one of more of the above. The cinema of Amitabh Bachchan was the resolution of the politics of status anxiety through cinema, the cinema which became both intensely philosophical and articulately political.

---

5 Ayan Rand. "Egalitarianism and Inflation" (1974) in Philosophy – Who Needs It. Signet. USA. 1982.Pp 120-122.

Politics and the Popular Culture

Popular culture is always political because of the resistances and the eventual adaptations it makes within a structure of social domination. John Fiske is very clear that while the popular culture operates within the framework of domination, it eventually makes it out in the world despite that domination. It is in its adaptations rather than in its open conflict that popular culture becomes political. Observers and scholars who are not 'fans' of popular culture and upon whom popular culture has no impact, insist that popular culture confirms stereotypes and upholds the status quo. What such scholars miss out really is the inner processes at work in the works of popular culture, where the domination is the given premise and the skirting around the domination is the resolution in which the hegemonic forces are beaten down. Since the status quo is only slyly evaded and not overtly challenged, it gives the impression that popular culture is not political.[1]

Scholars and journalists often say that the cinema of Amitabh Bachchan were influenced by the politics of its times, not noticing that cinema, especially popular cinema, has always

1 John Fiske. Understanding Popular Culture. Routledge. South Asian Publication. London. 2009. Pg 25.

been influenced by politics of its times. The cinema before Amitabh challenged the traditional society with the liberations promised by the Indian Constitution, while the cinema of Amitabh Bachchan challenged the State for belying its promises to the people liberated from traditions, but now thrown into the anonymity of the city to abound its pavements or live as its proletariat.

Amitabh's cinema appeared to be more political than the films which went before his era because he was a hero who existed at the divide of statuses; he lived in one while stepping over to the other, and in this change-over from one compartment of the society into the other, encountered several of those universes that define and hold together the structure of the society. The hero encountered clash of values, of morals, of law, codes of conduct, manner of speech, limits of legitimacy, the police, state, maternal authority and even God. The absent father motif in Amitabh's films is also political, because the absence of paternal authority leaves the individual free to step into his father's shoes, becoming the bread winner and the final authority over his own life.

The State

The State is the monopoly of force and this is why it must defend those it has disarmed from those who are yet to be stripped of the weapons that they hold. The State's prime duty is to protect its citizens against violence exerted by some elements in the society; if it cannot do so, it has no right to criminalise those who use violence as self-defense. This is the sum and substance of the hero's arguments in Amitabh's films. These arguments expand into discourses around law and jurisprudence.

Amitabh's films raised an important question; why was it that the State could not protect its own citizens from violence? According to the hero, this failure of the State lay in its address of economic inequalities in the society. In films before Amitabh Bachchan, the sources of violence were in status inequalities of the society, but with Amitabh and later heroes, the sources of violence came to reside almost exclusively in the economic inequalities. Violence was a means to maintain economic divides, deprive people of their fair rewards and prevent the meritorious from ascending to greater wealth. The ability of the State to prevent violence came to be intricately woven into the question of the State's relation to property. As long as the State did not address the issue of economic inequality, violence could not be eliminated from the system.

But why does the hero encounter violence in the first place? This is because he refuses to accept the oppression and counts himself not as a victim of the system but its ruler. Despite his poverty and destitution, the hero imagines that he can take hold of the system which exploits him so that he can undo its oppressive powers. The confidence to rule comes from a very superior understanding of the law and its paradoxes; the hero's actions are outcomes of his superior thought processes. The hero argues that the spirit of the law should empower everyone to participate equally in the development of the society; especially, the society should promote the talented, which the hero is. The talented individual changes the society's status quo when he breaks the social structure to emerge from its bottom rung into the upper echelons. He faces resistance from the incumbents of the position; this resistance feels like violence for the hero and his struggles against the entrenched privileges appears as violence in the eyes of the establishment.

Whose violence is the violence? The one who starts the chain, or the one who breaks the chain? The hero says that the law attacks those who break the chain of violence, one who uses violence to stall the violent and if the violence of the violent is ignored and the violence of the victim made in self-defense is taken as violence, then the law is being the protector of violence. If the law is violent, then the State that is supported by such law is also violent.

Negri says that the idea of peace is really not equilibrium but the complete ascendance of one kind of interest over the others.[1] In the Indian thought system, peace is the simultaneous fulfilment of every kind of interest in the society. The idea of the Indian *dharma* is the moral obligation which the ruler has over the protection of all kinds of diverse interests in the society both vis-à-vis the State as well as against one another. The hero in the films starring Amitabh Bachchan fights the system, its values

---

1 Antonio Negri. A Time for Revolution. Continuum. Bloomsbury. First South Asian Edition. New York. 2003. Pg 115.

and its logic rather than only an adversary; this makes his films change the power structure of the society and hence, makes them political.

Amitabh fights at two levels; one is with the villains just to get them out of the way, but the other is the ideological battle against the institutions. The hero argues that systems attack the aspiring meritorious people because the institutions are limited and constrained in their thoughts. The institutions are constrained because the ideas are rigid as they have failed to evolve with the changing reality of their times. The arguments of the hero then descends into the ideas of the universals, which do not contain the particulars but are imposed from the above on the society, since concepts which are not rooted within an empirical context tend to become reified and hence oppressive. These generalisations become hegemonic rules and which are repressive of the rhythm of everyday life. Law should be empowering by constantly responding to the objective reality, rather than become instruments of mindless disciplining. The rigidity of law and its callousness towards the society that can be traced to the State's support to the propertied class is the source of social conflict, which the hero feels must be overcome for a just society.

The Nation

I often read how the star of the Hindi film expresses the idea of the nation and of nationalism. I wonder how I missed the nation in the films and why is it that only the male stars are mentioned when one speaks of the nation? Where are the women? Frankly, I think that the idea of a nation cannot be expressed in pursuing everyday routine livelihoods, marriage and family, and this is exactly what the Hindi film does, because popular culture does so. The popular culture is about everyday life, writes John Fiske; it is about that life that you make into your own despite the fact that the coordinates of existence are shaped for you by those who are in power to control and command things. Within the capitalist apartment, yours is a small rental property but that is your home too. Popular culture is my home within a large house. The nation is that large house, popular culture is about the nation in the same way a tenant lives in homes not built by her.[1] Popular politics is about the nation, affiliations to teams in spectator sports lies in the nation, but popular cinema that pertains to life within the nation can only have the nation as the outer limits of the frames that provides meanings to the activities within the cinema. John Fiske contends that popular culture is everyday life and it is this position that is held through all the essays in the book.

1 John Fiske. Understanding Popular Culture. Routledge. New York. 2009. Pg 33.

The Hindi film addresses the nation as far as it is a part of everyday life and the outer limit of legitimate actions within which the social actor operates. In the context of India, the social traditions have always been grave impositions on freedom upon people, freedom that is so needed to participate in life. The idea of the Indian nation, as enshrined in its Constitution and as developed through a long drawn popular movement, in fact, attempts to subvert the social powers of tradition. For India, the nation is supposed to be a free for all public sphere that grants liberty equally to all. In my opinion, the Hindi film upholds the nation in that promise.

As long as the heroes confront the traditional powers which usually manifest in strict parents, mean relatives, sadist money lenders, and wicked landlords and wanton vamps striving to move past their stranglehold upon him, he may be said to be invoking the nation as an idea that recognises personal freedom from such oppression. In case of Amitabh Bachchan, things become different. His conflict is not with tradition as much as they are with the institutions which are the very products of modernity, especially when these institutions which are supposed to be expansive and enabling start reproducing similar disabilities as tradition. Institutions may favour the rich over the poor, may use similar class distinctions, and use nepotism against the meritorious candidates and other similar kinds of exclusionary practices. The hero's detractors are the avaricious builder, the gluttonous businessman, the scheming hotelier or simply the unscrupulous adventurer; these are all men who are the very products of modernity but belie its cause by creating exclusions in the society. The nation is contained in the hero's battles to win freedom for himself as a man who is not propertied but is deserving because he is meritorious. The hero invokes the nation as a superior set of morality which not only protects the deserving individual from the capricious rich, but also ensures that the State, through its institutions of law, protects the everyman.

The Family

Theodore Koditschek writes in his essay, *Genius and the Household Mode of Intellectual Production* in 1795 – 1885s that the genius is an exceptionally talented person who critiques the society, and in this critique, manifests his talents and belongs to the middle or the lower-middle-class family, and is determined to break the mould. This description suits the hero portrayed by Amitabh Bachchan very well. The genius is profoundly critical of his society because he is very aware of an alternative order. The new revolutionary, according to Koditschek, is not the artist, nor the poet, but the visionary who looks at the anomalies of the ideology, growing disparities, social and economic contradictions, and the requirements of the pragmatic life and the belied promises of the revolution. Such persons had no platform to showcase their work; in case of the films starring Amitabh, the cinema became such a platform and no wonder that the medium of cinema almost became an institution; the film business became an industry.[1]

The genius is a genius because s/he is at work. The work expresses the hero, his actions and activities are all that he has, and in his work, the hero is continually separated from home. The motifs of the orphan, the lost or even the dead father, the

1 Theodore Koditschek. "Genius and the Household Mode of Intellectual Production 1795-1885" in Journal of Social History. Volume 39. No 2. Winter 2005. OUP. pp 429-449.

disapproving mother, the errant brother which keep appearing in Amitabh's films, are strategies to separate the hero from his family and render him into a loner. The genius is always a loner. The separation between the hero and his family becomes the source of emotions throughout the film.

The separation of work from home and the worker from his family transforms the portrayal of the family from the site of reproduction into a machine for producing the worker. Not marriage but earning a living comes to be the central focus of the family.

In *Deewar*, the news of pregnancy of his girlfriend makes the hero surrender to the police, in *Trishul* the abandonment by his father makes the hero scorn the very institution of the family, in *Khuda Gawa* or *Aakhri Raasta*, his family is lost from him. But in *Khuddar* and *Hum*, he forfeited the joys of his life to look after his young siblings. When the family is thrust upon the hero, it becomes a responsibility, part of his activity or work. As a child, he becomes the breadwinner, or avows revenge upon those who harmed his father. The hero repeatedly steps into the shoes of his absent father, becomes the father and the protector himself. Koditscheck says that genius hero can barely afford the family, and this is why, looking after the family becomes such a task for the hero. Hence, the family is not something that the hero wants; the family is something which is thrust upon him like the burden of Sinbad.

The difficulty of raising a family and the need for the hero to be a loner in order to contemplate his vision throws him into a male bonding. Dual heroes, maintain the author, are essential in the life of the genius, and we do see that Amitabh's pairs are more spoken of in terms of his male co-star. The lady love is relegated into the background to show the hero's minimal attachment to reproduction – romance is at best a routine.

The family which is now suppressed out of the hero's life gets back at him in the form of the disciplining mother. She represents the establishment, and though a victim of the same powers of the society, she nonetheless endorses the values of the hegemonic powers. She disciplines her son if only to protect himself from his own passions, his impossible dreams of a better world. But his mission gets the better of himself; he is attached to his mother and to her, he wishes to return, only to be carried away with the calling of his own pilgrimage. Then he eventually returns home to die in his mother's lap, showing the impossibility of being at home. The lack of family becomes the homelessness of the hero and it also makes him into the worker who is irretrievably separated from home.

Mother

We started off our discussion by suggesting that Amitabh Bachchan was the concentration of individual powers to effect a change in his social status rather than being merely a problem-solving hero. He could change his social position by assuming a higher position of authority, wealth and status for himself as well as his family. In *Deewar*, *Trishul*, *Don* and many other films, he rises to higher social classes and because of this social mobility, the hero's relationship with his family changes. The family, in the Hindi formula film, contains the stock characters of the mother, usually an unmarried sister and a spoilt brother. The father is usually the villain who stands against the hero. The construction of the father in this way creates a space for the hero to rise into, in order to become the breadwinner himself. This may be a male fantasy to assassinate the father and take his place.[1]

The mother challenges the hero's selfishness, places a cap on his self-centeredness, which is needed if he is to rise up the social ladder through the dint of his merit. The mother has a very important role to play in Amitabh starrers, for she represents that morality which the hero wants to overcome and negate. The brother stands against the hero's missions, a game spoiler of sorts, sometimes bringing in the police as in *Deewar*, or embarrassing

1 Carl Jung. Aspects of the Masculine. Routledge. Special Indian Edition. London. 2003. Pg 18.

the hero as in *Parvarish* or *Satte Pe Satta*; and at other times, being trivial and interested in a life most ordinary, in comparison to the high life that the hero aspires for.

Upward social mobility requires investments on children; in Amitabh's films, it is the hero who gets the least of all resources. In *Deewar* and *Agneepath*, he becomes a child labourer in order to support his more ordinary brother; in *Khuddar* and *Hum*, he sacrifices all to bring up his brothers; in *Mahaan*, the less fortunate twin appears to be the more talented one. The lack of resources spent on the hero in comparison to what he brings gives the sentimental flavour to the hero. The principle emotions in an Amitabh Bachchan film is the ingratitude of the family, taking him for granted and the lack of appreciation for his efforts, which makes him extremely lonely. The principle motif of the family in Amitabh starrers is his loneliness among a family which never acknowledges his contribution nor appreciates his talents.

The hero is attached to his mother, but the mother is forever torn between the status quo and the change that her son brings about. The son fights for space in a system that resists the have nots to attain social status or to have equal opportunities to compete; the son fights for his due rewards in a system which guards the status quo by promoting and privileging the entrenched elites of the society. The hero clashes with the morality of his age and the law of his times, when he asks for a greater opening up of opportunities, for a more inclusive society. In this contest of morality between what is regarded as lawful and the apparent lawlessness of her son, the hero's mother stands against him for she fears for his life. There is a misunderstanding between the hero and his mother; his mother scolds him for his own good, the hero breaks law and places himself in danger for his mother's good. They work for each other's' good and in doing so, become enemies of each other. *Trishul*, seems to be an exception where the hero and his mother conspire together to take revenge against the father.

Masculinity

The cinema celebrates sexuality because the erotic is an important aspect of its aesthetic. The close up of bodies, the tracking of the nuances of their movements, the use of song and dance and the attainment of sublimity as ordained by the formula of the popular appeal, makes the erotic central to the popular cinema. Therefore, heterosexual attraction and then romance, followed by its fructification in marriage, is essential to the popular film of any language in India. Masculinity is as important as femininity, yet, analysts and scholars talk more of masculinity than of femininity, although we have enough of published articles which discuss the construction or the representation of women in cinema as being stereotyped to fit into the patterns of conformity in patriarchy. Men and women are represented distinctly in our cinema; they represent different flavours, and to say that women are cast as stereotypes of conformity to patriarchy, and that while the men are painted as its victors, women are constructed as its victims, is bad analysis.

How are women shown in the popular Hindi cinema? Women constitute the baseline on which the film rests; looked at carefully, the Hindi film is about women, the male activity gets meaning with respect to women. Raj Kapoor encounters Nargis as the epitome of virtue and good morality in many of their films together, Dev Anand is good or bad the way he 'delivers' to women, virtuous or vicious, Rajesh Khanna appears as the one who pleases a Sharmila Tagore or Asha Parekh. An honorable hero is one who treats women well, helps protect her boundaries in her moral integrity, lives up to her expectations of good life, while the villain is one who abrogates a woman's integrity.

Laura Mulvey's thesis that popular culture privileges the male gaze upon feminine bodies may not be applicable in case of India. Her theories are drawn from the context of the American popular culture which has a history and a sociology very different from that of India's[1] Amitabh Bachchan's films changed this orientation of the Hindi cinema and the hero, instead of protecting the woman's spaces, pushed the women out into the margins and emerged himself as the moral space that becomes the bounden duty for the State and the society at large to protect. In this avatar of the hero, we say that with Amitabh Bachchan, masculinity came to dominate the Hindi film, masculinity that wholly absorbed the requirements of femininity to be physically protected. Women were the moral centres, while the men were the centres of activity; in an Amitabh starrer, the hero became both; the moral centre as well as the action hero. The hero in the Amitabh starrers are very often children, the child taking over the physical vulnerability which women were subject to. The male activity finds a limit in the women who are the moral base of the films. In case of Amitabh Bachchan, it is the law and not the women who limit him, though in films like *Khoon Pasina*, *Ganga ki Saugandh*, *Suhaag* and even *Muqaddar Ka Sikandar*, Rekha as his heroine served the role of limiting and containing Amitabh's boundless exercise of will.

Men as action heroes in the age of Amitabh Bachchan, like Vinod Khanna and Shatrughan Sinha, started having missions rather than dreams, and were pilgrims or explorers than travelers. In the pre-Amitabh era, men and women were in the frame together; during the age of Amitabh, men tried hard to

---

1 Laura Mulvey. Visual Pleasure and Narrative Cinema. Screen Volume 16. No 4. 1975. Pp 6-18.

avoid women altogether. The famous song in *Kallicharan* sang by Lata Mangeshkar and lip synced by Reena Roy, 'Jaare Ja or Harjai' in which the heroine resents the fact that the hero does not care about her and how she is in utter despair over her unrequited love, expresses the masculinity of the hero and the femininity of the heroine. The women seem to start to develop a victim syndrome as the men turn into unapologetic and unnoticing oppressors of femininity.

In *Deewar*, Amitabh falls to his death only because the bar dancer, played by Parveen Babi, lures him and gets pregnant, and the hero, in the interests of his yet to be born child, surrenders to the police and is killed in the process. Amitabh's masculinity lies not in exercising his sexuality, but in refraining from sex altogether. His masculinity, in this sense, is the yogic masculinity which consists of abstinence. His aloofness, his ascetic pilgrimage, a clear separation between the comforts of the home that sometimes remain only a distant memory and the hardships of life, constitutes a version of masculinity which has almost no presence of a woman. Sunil Dutt and Dharmendra were brawny heroes; stronger and more macho than Amitabh Bachchan could ever be, because even in his deathly fights, Amitabh was never beefy and burly. He did not have the crudity nor the heftiness that often went with Sunil Dutt, Dharmendra or even with Shatrughan Sinha; instead, he exuded a certain cerebral refinement even when playing the role of a street goon, and his masculinity appears to come more from a wide-ranging vision, a sense of command over things, a strong acumen to get things going and a preparedness and planning that would precede his actions. Amitabh expressed no helplessness of his sexuality, no despair in the face of his sexual desire and instead, appeared to be in full command of his basic instincts. The command which Amitabh exuded as a hero over his thoughts and action and the certainty with which he pursued his goals, constitutes his masculinity.

Carl Jung's work on masculinity, says that the crux of masculinity is twofold, one is the hero and the other is the libido, and both are related to each other.[2] Man becomes a hero when he detaches from his mother; with the constant fear of incest hovering over him, the hero sets out on a path of his own to increase progressively the distance between his mother and him. Masculinity in India does not exactly follow this path, since the passage through the stages of life is clearly separated in the form of ritualised interventions. However, masculinity in the Hindi film pertains to growing into an adult in the public sphere of a modernising ancient tradition. The hero grows up and moves out of his home in search of livelihood, which includes employment and finding a girl to marry and it is then that he exercises his agency by limiting his will, sharpening his reason and organising his action and overcomes his obstacles. He becomes a person from merely someone who existed, and this transformation constitutes his masculinity. Masculinity, in the Hindi film, is a process, rather than an end product, and the process has both the discovery as well as the deployment of the libido and the exercise of restraint.

Amitabh Bachchan, when considered from the above model, emerges into masculinity; in most cases as a mere child. We may say that masculinity is imposed upon him before puberty, for he often loses his father and alights on the vast and hostile world to earn for his family. He becomes the breadwinner and forsakes his childhood. Amitabh's world is hostile, for his father has been murdered and his enemies rule the roost. The hostility of the world may well be the quality of the objective reality that a child labourer faces, because in order to enter the work world, the child is snatched away from her family, her moorings, her home and subjected to the discipline of work and routine, and irrespective of whether the employer is kind or cruel, the world is hostile for the child labour for the simple reason that it uproots her. Amitabh as a hero grows up by forgetting a lot, the repression of instincts becomes an act of will turned inwards and the power which is

2 Carl Jung. Aspects of the Masculine. Routledge. Special Indian Edition. London. 2003. Pg 18, para 456.

required constitutes the masculinity of the hero. Then there is a power turned outwards and which is his ability to fight. This is an addition to the qualities of the hero which are his ability to think through things, reasoned restraint and strategic planning. Javed Akhtar of the Salim Javed duo, the creators of the image of Amitabh Bachchan, was a fan of Dev Anand, a hero who is well known for his sharp problem-solving mind, using the minimum of brawn. In plain sight, it might appear that Salim Javed just added a physical prowess to Dev Anand to convert him into Amitabh, and with this invented an appealing and effectual libido in the form of fights; but this was not all[3]. Amitabh worked not only out of a clever mind but out of a wise mind, for no hero has ever come before him or after him who had a large understanding of his personal predicament as one that originated in the structure of the State and in its legal system, in its values and morals, in its social conventions and power struggles. The holism of Amitabh's vision that gave him a sense of power and authority over the world at large constitute the crux of his masculinity. The hero is the one who is extremely focused, determined, and capable of both, unassailable arguments as well as invincible blows.[4]

---

3 Javed Akhtar. Classic Legends. Season 2 Episode 3. Dev Anand. Epic Channel. https://www.youtube.com/watch?v=gbxiY2ZzmSw&t=42s

4 For the Indian ethos, masculinity is in fact not libido, it is agency, effectuality, ability to command things, ability to change things, wisdom to do the right things, will to bring justice, reason to see the good. Libido is regarded in the Indian system of thought as juvenile simplicity, something that braced Birju, the male hero played by Sunil Dutt in Mother India or the young Lord Krishna in his days of dalliance with the women of Vrindavan. In his avatar as Narayana, Krishna is suave, officious and full of material comfort; his authority seems to have tempered his need for libido, which inhered him while he was still a child. Arjuna and Ram are masculine as epic heroes for they are noble, skilled, intelligent, determined, focused, ethical and strategic warriors. Bhim, another epic hero is bucolic and direct, and though a hefty fellow, is no more masculine nor more effective than Ram or Arjuna. and Lord Shiva, on the other hand is the ultimate virile on account of his panoptic sway over the world, his patience, his asceticism, and his being above the material world and hence above libido.

The masculinity discussed above braces the image of Amitabh Bachchan as Salim Javed created it. But when we come to the later films of Amitabh Bachchan starting from *Lawaaris* in 1981 and *Coolie* in 1982, the hero has turned misogynist. The man with a holistic vision of the world becomes resentful and vengeful; while in *Deewar*, the hero's angst was against the structure, and though he argues his head off with his brother who upholds the exploitative structure, the hero realises that he punishes villains because the law is blind to the exploitation that systems promote. By the time *Coolie* is made, the hero has become resentful towards incumbents of positions and he seems to have lost his holism or his logical thinking and instead, assigns the woes of his life to some rich guy. It is in *Coolie* that Amitabh emerges on screen as a veritable abuser of women in the way he treats the heroine, in the way he swears revenge on a woman because he is angry with the men of her family and how he collects his fellow railway porters and attacks the homes of his employer in the manner of the Bolshevik Revolution shown in the film *Dr Zhivago* or in the D.W.Griffith's film, *Birth of a Nation,* or in the likes of what happened in the rule of the mob in the *Reign of Terror* post the French Revolution. Masculinity thus changes from a revolution into a street fight, fought on face to face, over bodies of women and away from the public sphere, because it is no longer a matter of debates, or the law courts, or even of arguments, but of heckling, milling, mobbing, raising an angry crowd, exciting people and inciting them to violence by rabble rousing speech.

The masculinity of the hero in *Coolie* and thereafter in the films of Manmohan Desai which were to follow namely *Toofan* and *Mard*, are abusive of women. The hero insults women who are unchaperoned in public spaces, contemptuous of women in charge of their own lives. Such masculinity inheres a hero who has lost his productive capabilities of work, one who merely protests perhaps in order to divert attention from the lack of creativity in him, and this is why he needs politics and bargains from the position of a victim. The *Coolie* trilogy, namely *Toofan* and *Mard*, is a far cry from *Deewar* or *Trishul*, *Sholay* or *Don*, when the hero is capable of changing his social status through sheer hard work.

In *Coolie*, the hero ceases to be alone; though he is separated from his family, he nonetheless belongs to a 'cadre', that of the organised union of railway porters. The organisation has structured his work and the scope for individual work is limited; it is the organisation that contains him, routinising his work and capturing his masculinity not as a worker but as an organisation man in which his effectuality lay in arranging mob attacks rather than arguing on reason. Such masculinity as shown in *Coolie*, places the male in his cadre, in a kind of a hostel, or a barrack where women are literally not allowed entry and the male can protect his purity by only spurning the woman. The asceticism which Amitabh showed in the 1970's now becomes monastic in the 1980's, and in which women are constructed as leading to sin and being totally antithetical to the purity of maleness; masculinity, thus, gets constructed as that which is abusive of women.

There are thus three constructs of masculinity; one that inheres in heroes before Amitabh Bachchan that pertains to personal style, fashion, restraint, values, judgments, loyalties to reason rather than faith. Within Amitabh Bachchan, there are two further constructs, one by Salim Javed and the other by Manmohan Desai. The former is effectual and ascetic, lonesome and meditative, whose actions are born of visions of vitality. The latter is reactionary, spontaneous, punitive and born out of ties of loyalties towards a community. The former is the productive man while the latter is a vagabond, alienated and thrown off any organised employment. The shift in masculinity takes place with a shift in the productive opportunities of the Indian society, as the absorptive powers of the Indian economy reduces, leaving less scope for the genius and less opportunities of employment. The changes in Amitabh's masculinity over the years shows the decline of the Indian society's employment scenario, decline in the productive powers which we today see manifested in the decline in industries and the manufacturing sector, farmer and student suicide, violence against women and in road rage and mayhem.

The City

The Hindi film loves the city as much as it loves its open landscapes, the valley of flowers; the lush of grains in fields, verdant forests, gushing waterfalls and its snow-covered mountain slopes. The natural landscape gives bodies on the screen scope for free movements, the visual stimulus of the open spaces relaxes the mind and provides an opportunity for music to roll on and attain long and high notes. But the city provides the rhythm, the feel of speed, the excitement of newer levels of tactile agitation, newer apprehensions and anticipations of heady experiences. The city is a space of opportunities but also of selfishness and soullessness, of more work and less leisure and because of its anonymity, also a space for personal freedom. It is in cities that those who are lost are found again and it is in the cities that the Divine reveals impossible miracles. The city helps the poor see the palace and the city also throws the rich into destitution; the city is the place to romance, the city is also the place to die. It appears that the city and not the countryside has played a more vital role in the Hindi cinema; whether Raj Kapoor's coming to senses in *Shree 420*, or finding his father in *Awara*, whether it is Dilip Kumar's role as Bholenath in *Bairaag*, who comes to redeem himself in the city, or in *Pyasa* in which the life of a poet is essayed on the cruel calculativeness of the city, or Sharmila Tagore who is abused in the city in *Aradhana* or in

Amar Prem. In purely romantic films such as *Bobby* or Shammi Kapoor's films, love flourishes in the bounty of nature amidst the riot of colours of the spring but in films which must convey social conflicts and personal struggles, the city must be the backdrop. Needless to say, the city, as a site of strife and struggle, becomes the defining background to Amitabh's films.

The hero traverses the pavements of the city and abounds in its palaces; the city covers his biography from rags to riches but more than that, from the victim of oppression into one who emerges into that great power himself; that power which is so powerful that it can destroy all and yet its possessor, the hero, is so restrained that he desists from exercising his power. The acquisition of power and then the control of will to unleash it creates a tension which is borne well by the clank and clamour of the city. In the films of Manmohan Desai, especially the ones after *Coolie*, namely *Toofan* and *Mard*, the hero emerges in unpeopled geographies among the remnants of feudal lords, hoary colonisers and strange enemies of unspecified people. The hero's battles are all won and now he must find larger and larger enemies who would challenge him to duels; the villains become grander and the hero fiercer, both needing the open spaces again to give their bodies greater scope of movements just as the romantic films would do. Violence becomes the new erotica in Manmohan Desai's cinema and the hero moves out of the city limits. But Amitabh's is mainly an image which is contained in the city.

George Simmel, the sociologist of the city, in his essay on the Metropolis and Mental Life says that the city throws up a challenge for the mental life of humans, for it is here that overwhelmed by the urban civilisation, the individual seeks to find herself as an autonomous being[1]. The city has the capability of wrenching out individuals from their moorings in their traditions and social ties that bear these traditions and places

1 George Simmel, 'Metropolis and Mental Life'. 1903 in Gary Bridge and Sophie Watson ed. The Blackwell City Reader. Oxford and Walden, MA Wiley Blackwell. 2002.

them in associative relationships those which are contingent and likely to be momentary only; the relationships, those which a city allows, are those which are built upon certain levels of exchanges, meeting of minds, and indeed intensifications of certain aspects of one's persona. The city cannot contain the whole; it alienates, it divides personalities, intensifies some attributes and represses some others. For Amitabh Bachchan, the divisive character of the city worked very well to repress his softer emotions and bring out the harder qualities in him. No wonder then *Don* was so vital; Don was the epitome of the hard hearted, sharp brained and lethal, while Vijay, a look alike, was his lost self and throughout the film, the lost self runs to access its projected image, namely Don. The city was used to its fullest for the purposes of this movie. In *Deewar*, the hero comes to the city to lose his childhood and to be forced into becoming an adult and the breadwinner of his family. The city's hugely accentuated architectures, the tall buildings, the flyovers, the temple at one corner from where the road parts into a giant Y never to meet again, the imposing ships at the docks, the shrill siren, the rushing trucks and the railway tracks on which slums have piled on, reflect the mind of the hero, ambitious, struggling to reach the heights of material wealth and bereft of the comeliness that braced him in childhood. The city in *Deewar* is discontinuous with his life, for here he has lost his father, quarrels with brother, falls out with his mother and 'picks' up his family on a wayside bar. All trajectories are lost in the city, newer ones are formed in unexpected ways. The city fragments but intensifies as well.

Despite death and destruction, Amitabh is the hero who the city creates as its victor, one who finds a new autonomy and holism while struggling through his own fragments; he is not like Guru Dutt or like Raj Kapoor, who the city dismantles and depresses. The city makes Amitabh the fighter that he is; the hero accepts the reification of the city, acknowledges that its main concentration lies in material power whose foundation lies upon a systematic exploitation of humans. He rises with his intellect to conquer the laws that govern the city till the point he becomes its law. In *Agneepath*, his near fatal injuries cause riots in the city, for he has emerged as the parallel city: redistributing its wealth, curbing its oppressors. The city looks upon him as its God; a long way from *Deewar* in which the hero challenges God as one who is so dead in the city. The hero played by Amitabh accepts his fate, in the partition of the self; he casts his heart aside and rules ruthlessly through reason. He discovers a whole new set of capabilities, learns how to bargain, learns to earn money through the deployment of his labour and learns how to concentrate and focus. The city does not merely break him, it provides him with both, a challenge and new vigour to pull himself up into an integrated whole through the exercise of his new found sense of agency. The city overwhelms the hero only to be conquered by him and perhaps even to surrender to him.

The city is a source of anxiety of Indians across the social milieu, because the modern city is a product of colonialism, and in the process of Independence, which is decolonialism, one must struggle to integrate the city in one's life. The city is at once the phantom of impersonality, one who's imposing architecture and unfamiliar organisation of space makes one from the village look foolish. *Jamaibabu*, a silent film made out of Calcutta in 1934, brings out the harassment of a villager when he comes to the city, because of its layout and architecture that organises life completely differently to which a villager is used to. In *Namakhalal*, a similar fate awaits Amitabh Bachchan who comes fresh from the village to find strange doors, strange lights, strange spaces, strange women and very strange humans, though he very quickly learns its ways and starts to enjoy its privileges. The city in the sociology of history helped the Indians overcome caste barriers, liberate its women, promote individual talents, and create opportunities for the nuclear family to live in comfortable seclusion enjoying the fruits of material culture more exclusively. The city, thus, cannot be only the alter ego of humans, it cannot merely overpower; indeed, the city must become an opportunity, and this is exactly what Amitabh Bachchan, as the hero of his films, successfully did.

There have been films in which Amitabh leaves the city to go into the countryside. In *Kabhie Kabhie,* he moves into a mining town, in *Kala Paththar* he exiles himself in a colliery, in *Satte Pe Satta* he lives in a sprawling farmland, in *Sholay* he moves out into a secluded village. In times when he does this, he travels to discover more of himself, in privacy. These are the moments when he finds himself unable to settle the confusions of his mind, he moves away into states of non-thinking. In such moments, he turns into his non being, a state of suspended existence. These are the moments of silences of the hero, like the pause in the music, a postponement of rhythm. These then become moments of self-renewal, both for his image as well as for his viewers, for both of whom his interrupted victories could have been exhausting.

The Den and the Temple

In the city, the hero moves between two interesting locations; one is the temple and the other is the den. The den is sometimes also the bar. Lots of stuff happens to the hero at the bar; it is mostly here that he meets the women of his life, women who are fugitives of law as much as he is, women who are invariably not the homely ones. These women taint him, forcing him into commitments that pull him into temptations, often away from home. The temple is, on the other hand, his roots, the place that pulls him back home. The temple is the epicenter of the hero, the den is the outer limit, between these two points, the hero places all his activities; being dragged to the circumference and pulled back into the centre.

In *Deewar*, the temple and the den are very clearly etched out. There are two kinds of temples, one where God lives and the other is the home where his mother is. The den is the one of Peter, of Dawar and the bar where he meets Anita, his love interest. In *Zanjeer*, his temple is his home, the one that Jaya decorates, while the den is the one in which Sher Khan arranges a musical or in which Teja lives and parties. In *Amar Akbar Anthony*, the Church is the temple of God while Anthony, the hero, runs the bar himself. In *Kasme Vaade*, the hero comes in from the den to the temple, the home of his look alike. The two spaces enclose a ground which the hero covers in his act of covering, which according to Deleuze, constitutes the movement of cinema.[1] These two spaces also become two sides of the hero's persona; the den represents his uprootedness from his moorings, the distance he has come from his childhood values, while the temple returns us back to his base, his roots, the point from which he began it all and to where he intends to return.

Amitabh's image needs the temple badly; for it is the roots that give a balance to the character who explodes monotonically by promising that one who constantly evolves must end his journey and return. Death accomplishes this and *Deewar* does this best because the hero dies in the temple in his mother's lap. In *Sholay*, he dies in the presence of his love interest as well as in his friend's arms.

1 Gilles Deleuze. Cinema 1. First South Asian Edition. Continuum. London. 1986. Pg 1.

Post-Amitabh Era

In the era during which Amitabh came back from politics to films to refresh his position in cinema, there was a crisis in his image perhaps due to the brief break he took in politics. Amitabh being in politics was not merely a film star being in Parliament, for Nargis and Prithviraj Kapoor have been there before, but in fact, Amitabh was an elected member of the Lok Sabha, while film stars before him were nominated to the upper house. Politics represented an end of the journey, or a materialisation of the promises of Amitabh's image. The image of Amitabh Bachchan is intensely political; he is always arguing against the State, against law, heavily discoursing on morality and jurisprudence and hence, politics was the natural maturity of his image. When he became an elected member of parliament and a close aide to the prime minister of the country, his image was fructified in what is deserved. Politics complete the logical possibilities of the image of Amitabh Bachchan. Politics exhausted Amitabh's possibility and so, when he returned to films again, people could not pick up the strands afresh; it was as if the fans thought that the journey has already found its end, so now what?

Amitabh's image in this period was an exhaustion of his stardom, playing roles of men who had quite lived their lives, been there and done that but linger on to tie some lose ends. This was a period when two stars rose and ruled over the viewers, one was Anil Kapoor and the other was Govinda. Govinda and Amitabh starred together in *Bade Miyan Chhote Miyan*, a remake of Shakespeare's Comedy of Errors, but Amitabh and Anil Kapoor have practically no memorable work together.

Anil Kapoor's image is defined by his film *Mr India* in 1984, after which he became a huge star. Irreverent and with sarcastic humour, Anil Kapoor acted in the role of a man who could by some magic, become invisible, and in a state of invisibility, he heckled the bad guys. After *Mr India's* success, invisibility came to inhere the image of Anil Kapoor. Amrish Puri who played the role of the villain, Mogambo, emerged in visual grandeur, to compensate the hero's invisibility. Anil Kapoor remains largely underground, slightly unnoticed, an underdog, and the back bencher in *Ram Lakhan*, *Tezaab* and *Kishen Kanhaiya*, and even perhaps in *Parinda*, and in this invisibility, he ruled all through the 1990's. Anil Kapoor broke the need of Hindi films to pursue ideology, or to have a central purpose, and brought about lightness in the Hindi film, which may have been a relief to the viewers after the intensity of Amitabh Bachchan.

Anil Kapoor had none of the high sounding and heavy weather arguments of Amitabh Bachchan; he was more of the 'little guy' and he was the hero when politics was increasingly taking the shape of popular culture and descending into cinema, rather than cinema expanding to absorb politics. Much like Jeetendra, Anil Kapoor is a star who can slip easily into different moulds very easily. He is a shape shifter of sorts. He turned out to be very useful at times when the Hindi film was in a state of vacuum; Amitabh been displaced and no star really replacing him. If there was truly a legatee of Amitabh Bachchan, it was perhaps Govinda.

Govinda was the other superstar in this post-Amitabh period; while Anil Kapoor resisted typecasting, Govinda was a genre unto himself. If Amitabh's was an era, Govinda's films were completely different genre, and while the genre did not consume the whole of Bollywood, it nonetheless made a distinct and a specialised line of production possible, which had its distinct coterie of producers and directors and distributors and music makers and choreographers. As business, Govinda was the most viable model in the post-Amitabh era; the most bankable investment.

Govinda was a laugh riot and a scandal. He wooed two women at the same time, pretending to be two persons, cared for none, respected none, a man who was one of the industry's finest dancers. Irreverent, made fun of all and most of all of himself, Govinda was nihilistic; nothing could stand in seriousness before him. Govinda's dance with minimal body movement that picked up even the slightest beat from tunes, his utterly expressive face that showed how much he enjoyed being himself, created a whole new genre of Hindi film around the star. Govinda's co-star had to fall in line with Govinda, he was the style, he was the montage and he was the script. Amitabh and Govinda acted in *Bade Miyan Chhote Miyan* together and Amitabh, also known for his side-splitting hilarious comedy, was actually seen to be struggling to be accommodated in the same screen as Govinda. The more recent Salman Khan and Govinda starrer, *Partner* did not do as expected because each could not be accommodated to the rhythm of the other. Govinda stands tall alone; his pace and tone is set so finely that no other kind of body movement except his own can be accommodated in that space.

Amitabh as a Media Construct

Towards the close of the 1990's, Amitabh Bachchan, the invincible hero, the hero who is associated with the Mammon, fell into a financial disaster with the newly-formed entertainment company, namely the ABCL, going bankrupt. In his darkest hours, Amitabh was on the anvil of losing everything including the home he stayed in, and with ageing and ill parents to look after, he was almost going to be shelterless. On one of such days, he walked into Yash Chopra's office asking the director, who was responsible for directing films such as *Deewar* and *Kabhie Kabhie*, to give him a job. Yash Chopra's production, *Mohabbatein*, was made in this way.[1] By this time, Yash Chopra was cultivating Shah Rukh Khan and he was the reigning superstar of the moment and not only did Amitabh get cast opposite Shah Rukh, but the script was such that Shah Rukh was to castigate Amitabh in the film and demolish the image that he had held for so long. Amitabh Bachchan took all of this in and constantly opened himself to such demolitions in *Veer Zaara* as well and many films that followed. It was really

1 Amitabh Bachchan's own accounts. See http://indiatoday.intoday.in/story/amitabh-bachchan-ranbir-kapoor-failure-ae-dil-hai-mushkil/1/815944.html

not until *Sarkar* that Amitabh was once again rediscovered and reinstated as an action hero, but that superstardom by which he ruled over an entire era was definitely over.

Post 2000, Amitabh worked not for fame but for survival. In the words of Charles Dickens, 'these were the best of times and the worst of times' for Amitabh. The worst because he had to work really hard at an age when he should have ideally retired and the best because it was for the first time that Amitabh in real life did what he would do in his films, which is to work his way up into the palace from the pavement. For his purpose, he now chose the media, that very media which during his heydays as the superstar had castigated, defamed and demolished him. The entire episode of Amitabh's involvement in the Bofors case was a media construct, a creation of some vengeful scribes who Amitabh's evasion of the press had annoyed. The media punched him badly, and Amitabh came up with the statement that it was like being raped. Ever since the Bofors episode, Amitabh has truly lived like a victim: jumpy, ever alert, devastated and never really that cocky and confident that he once used to be. He is ever conscious should anyone still think that he was truly the villain who sold the nation. His relations with the Gandhi family broke, and he constantly tried to balance one kind of political patronage with others.

From 2000 till the present, Amitabh has become a media-created celebrity image, famous because we see more and more of him everywhere. Ever careful about his privacy, Amitabh revealed himself more and more and the YouTube is full of parties in his home, his poses with his grandchildren, the insides of his living room and shots of him stirring Horlicks in the kitchen; we seem to have seen enough of Amitabh. He writes his blog regularly which are rather ordinary with readers equally mediocre.[2]

He endorses endless brands and products and hosted the television show *Kaun Banega Crorepati*. As a host of the show, he

---

2 Daniel J Boorstin. The Image – A Guide To Pseudoevents in America, Vintage. New York. 1992.

proved his mettle again and perhaps took his revenge on Shah Rukh Khan by completely overshadowing him as an anchor. As an anchor of the show, Amitabh had to interact with thousands of participants, and in each case, he became an overwhelmed fan of the quizzard opposite him. For the few minutes that Amitabh sat opposite the participant, he became large eyed, ever inquisitive, highly curious and deeply interested in knowing everything about these normal people from all walks of life. Shah Rukh Khan could never really be Amitabh Bachchan because the former could never get over the fact that he was the star and not the one opposite him. Self-dissolution, self-abnegation is an achievement that requires a far higher level of empathy and intelligence and this simple straight set game between the two makes me unabashedly think of Amitabh Bachchan as the winner.

Javed Akhtar's Fears

Javed Akhtar is a lot on the television these days. Apart from a channel dedicated to Urdu poetry on Tata Sky, he also speaks about cinema in a programme called *Jaane Pehchaane* on the Epic Channel. In these discussions on cinema, Javed Akhtar very carefully avoids discussing Amitabh Bachchan, an image which he structured and which many others have layered. There is a very clear reason for this avoidance, and which is, I suspect, an innate fear in him that did he and Salim Khan, in the innocent enthusiasm of their youth, create an image of the hero as a fascist? Fascism is rocking the world today in its form of Islamic fundamentalism, racism in America and the right wing politics in India, and it is entirely possible that the sensibilities of the cinema has translated into the politics of the present.

There are many areas of commonality between Amitabh's image in cinema and the fascist imagination in politics. Fascist politics imagines a strong individual who can invade and take over the institutions of administration, whose will becomes the law and whose visions become the rule. Such an individual is also an ascetic, never found to be selfish and indeed when it was rumoured that Amitabh had taken money on the Bofors deal, the disappointment with his fans was very great because it made him appear as a selfish consumerist. Truly the hero's assertion in *Kaalia* in 1981 in which he says that the line begins wherever he is standing is a fascist assertion. *Kaalia*, a relatively minor film directed by Tinnu Anand who also directed the blockbuster *Shahenshah* post Amitabh's stint in politics in 1988, are both rather fascist. So are films of Manmohan Desai from *Coolie* in 1982 onwards. Javed Akhtar is not too wrong in avoiding the discussion of Amitabh in such sensitive times.

But there is a crucial difference between the romantic individual of Frank Kermode and the fascist.[1] The romantic individual is an autonomous being, wholly in command of his life, so rational that he can originate rules and laws through the first principles; he is law unto himself, self-absorbed and internally integrated. He is the source of order; he not only can direct his own life but he can also change the material conditions of his existence. There is yet another category of personality and which is the inner directed individual of David Reisman.[2] This kind of an individual is autonomous, effective, can bring about a change the level of technology in the society and one who is self-motivated, self-driven and self-disciplined, though rigid at times. Both the romantic image and the inner directed man, both examples of the Hegelian 'Spirit' have apparent resemblances with the fascist individual. But there is a very important difference between a fascist and an individual who exercises her agency. The differences are as follows.

The hero as portrayed by Amitabh Bachchan is angry with the system because of its inherent paradox; on the one hand democracy is supposed to enable everyone and ensure equal opportunities for all, but on the other hand, the law protects those who oppress and exploit others. When the hero bargains with the state, he does not look at his own powers vis-à-vis the institutions,

---

1 Frank Kermode. The Romantic Image. Routledge. South Asian Edition. 2002. The romantic individual is an artist in isolation and not a control freak. The fascist personality very well etched by Theodore Adorno, Authoritarian Personality is the one who is comforted in a herd rather than in isolation.

2 David Reisman. The Lonely Crowd –A Study of the Changing American Character. Yale University Press. Yale. USA. 1950. Pg 9.

but worries for the system as a whole, which might restrict its own growth prospect by being partisan and partial. Amitabh, as a hero, wants to break the status quo, not to place himself in the superior position of his class enemy, but the redistribution of power is a means to free the meritorious from social oppression so that he may contribute meaningfully for raising the levels of the entire society to newer levels. Amitabh's desire for equality underlies a desire for growth; and not for a mere swapping of positions between the privileged and the usurper.[3]

The fascist person, on the other hand, merely seeks to displace the ones who are well-ensconced in the society so that she may have her wealth, wear her clothes, and look like her. There is both a flavour of impersonation as well as imitation in its politics. The equality that the fascist wants is for herself; she may only be using equality for the mere effect, for all that a fascist person wants is to be like the elite of the society, but she will use every force to prevent anyone else displacing her in the manner she has displaced the entrenched class in the society. The fascist has little idea or imagination of growth and this is why while she may attack the institution, she has no capacity for building these as instruments for growth. In a sharp contrast to the fascist mind, Amitabh as the hero shows an enormous sense of the future and because of this imagines an entire order in which the material conditions from which oppression emanates are eliminated. Fascism has no script for changing the underlying material causes of social anomalies, Amitabh's discourses have clear causations with clarity of connections between the ends and means.

The will of the fascist is only to replace herself in the position of the incumbent, but not to allow those below her to arrive in her place. I think that this is where Amitabh's discourses are totally contrary for the hero speaks of laws and ethics, as those which facilitate merit across social classes and make social

---

3 T.W. Adorno, Else Frenkel-Brunswik, Daniel J. Levinson and R. Nevitt Sanford, The Authoritarian Personality, Studies in Prejudice Series, Volume 1 Harper & Brothers, Copyright American Jewish Committee, USA. 1950.

class irrelevant where equality of social opportunities are concerned. The fascist has no discourse of a general equality of opportunity, and claims only a space for herself in the scheme of things, without an adequate understanding of exclusions and the possible transformations in material reality in order to be inclusive. Amitabh's discourses are universal and inclusive; the fascist labels to break universals and excludes via those labelling. Amitabh, as a hero, fights labels, categories which are imposed upon people from above as he fights not at the demagogical level but at the dialogical one in which he constantly makes a case for laws to emanate from the lived-in reality of people. The fascist is anxious for her own status and therefore is too limited to develop holistic thought systems conceptualised by Salim Javed in their construction of the hero.

Javed Akhtar is safe. He need not worry.

A Divided House

Amitabh Bachchan has a strange way of fighting with his benefactors and despite being a man of long-held memories in his films, he seems to have very little remembrance of the steps he climbed to reach the pinnacle. In the heydays of his stardom, he nearly abandoned Salim Javed and Yash Chopra while cultivating Manmohan Desai. He had earlier cold-shouldered Prakash Mehra for Yash Chopra. He then cultivated a slew of directors over his favourites so that he could be free from the influential ones. He fought with his political family, the Gandhis and Amar Singh, who helped tide him over his deepest crisis in life. He seeks political patronage once from the Shiv Sena, and at other times from the Samajwadi Party, and then openly defects to the adversaries of his political benefactors, the BJP. Amitabh was said to be in love with Rekha who he never acknowledged and has not been too good to his wife, Jaya either leaving the latter progressively cantankerous and downright scurrilous if one goes by the YouTube videos.[1]

Dharmendra, Shatrughan Sinha, Salim Khan, Rishi Kapoor all have one thing to say and which is that Amitabh has never acknowledged them for their contributions in his career. Truly, the above mentioned have had important roles to play in the making of Amitabh Bachchan as a megastar and one wonders

1 See links https://www.youtube.com/watch?v=Fv9LpMZhQ44 or https://www.youtube.com/watch?v=jFKBa5bBdeM

why Amitabh never spoke about these people who helped him rise; his accounts are always of himself and his parents; even Jaya Bhaduri who had a vital and in many ways a sly role to play in 'setting up' Amitabh into Hrishikesh Mukherjee's heart by displacing Rajesh Khanna from the directors mind space, finds no mention in his reminiscences of success. I have also wondered whether or not Parveen Babi's allegation of Amitabh trying to kill her, were all completely out of place, if there was not already some hope which were raised in her by something in Amitabh's behavior towards her. He has been rude to and dismissive of his scribes, Khalid Mohammad and Rauf Ahmed, the two who wrote insightfully and poetically about him and were widely read by his fans in the early days of Amitabh Bachchan. Their contributions towards creating a discourse and hence, a curiosity about Amitabh Bachchan in the press, cannot be gainsaid.

Yet, he has been extremely caring of his parents, and a patient parent to his children. He is an indulgent father and nothing shows it better than in the utter contentment in the face of his children, especially when they are with him. He is fond of and caring towards his daughter-in-law, Aishwarya Rai and they have an endearing relationship with each other. Aishwarya, albeit in pictures and videos, seems to suggest that in her, Amitabh has found a genuine friend, for she is a topper in academics, in beauty pageant contests and in winning awards. He however has issues with her not always obeying the Bachchan household ritual of having meals together, which might be her routine or a way of avoiding her in-laws, as many young wives do, especially during meals. Amitabh is a person who does not carry anyone with himself. He may give himself wholly to the other person; loving, caring, nurturing, protecting, fighting and sacrificing, but refuses to carry anyone as his companion. Amitabh is a loner.

The industry says that Amitabh creates a high wall around him into which are privileged only his children, his parents, wife and some close friends, and even friends like Amar Singh may find themselves out on the road pretty soon. The high wall, which Amitabh calls as his privacy, is barely there and there is not much to be seen inside this wall. Amitabh, who post his political and financial debacle sought out the media badly to prop up his image, is not really publicity shy. If he does indeed put up a wall then it is to take rest, collect himself up, gather his focus and recoup his energies for the next performance. Indeed, the vanity van which is something which everyone carries around these days was started in the industry first by Amitabh Bachchan, perhaps due to his touchiness about the toilets and also the need for him to have home cooked food always.

Amitabh's failures, once in politics and the other time in business, have surprised me. His films have been political, the ideologies he has articulated are intensely political, and the image he projected are political as well. In his brief stint in politics, he made two major contributions; one was the idea of Rs 1 crore in those days, for each Member of Parliament, to be spent on the constituency for its development and the other was to raise, albeit in his interviews about his experiences about the Lok Sabha constituency of Allahabad, the issue of toilets. Jaya was very vocal of how women in the villages had to wait till dusk in order to relieve themselves. The present Prime Minister, Narendra Modi, must have taken it very seriously in order to have the construction of toilets inside every home as part of the Swachh Bharat Mission.

Amitabh Bachchan wanted the Hindi film industry to have the status of an industry, because once this was done, the industry would be more organised and will be subject to the various rules of employment like insurance and health cover as well as exemptions on profits. This, however did not happen. But Amitabh, in order to withstand the possible onslaught of the foreign media on the Indian industry in the aftermath of the economic liberalisation, decided to float his own entertainment company. Conceptually, the company was too large; Amitabh Bachchan is too much of a loner to handle work with so many people, and despite his meticulous attention in household matters, his capabilities fell short of handling the details of large finances. By the time the corporation, namely the ABCL, or Amitabh Bachchan Corporation Limited happened, Amitabh had fallen out with his younger brother, Ajitabh, alias Bunty. This was a major loss, especially since it was Ajitabh who is mainly said to have handled all his finances during his stardom.

Amitabh's Entitlements

Amitabh Bachchan used to bear a certain sense of entitlement about him in his early days of stardom. He came from a middle-class family but one which was well-established and which seemed to have improved its social status over the years. His father was Harivanshrai Bachchan, a poet, a teacher of English literature at the Allahabad University and a doctorate holder from Cambridge and eventually member of the Rajya Sabha. He was the winner of the Sahitya Akademi Awards and served in the Ministry of External Affairs for the promotion of Hindi. He was particularly close to the then Prime Minister, Pandit Jawaharlal Nehru and to Indira Gandhi. Teji was a Sikh who was raised in Lahore, one of pre-Independence India's most cultural cities. She taught Psychology in Lahore's DAV College when she married Harivanshrai. She was instrumental in getting Harivanshrai Bachchan into the glitterati, the literary and the political high circles. Teji was instrumental in getting Amitabh and his younger brother, Ajitabh into the residential school in which Rajiv Gandhi and Sanjay Gandhi studied, and it is here that they were in company of the political elite of the country.

Amitabh started his career in Kolkata. Kolkata was then a city of high fashion and cosmopolitanism. In this city, he was introduced to the social elite, the culture of clubs and parties. He was active as an amateur stage actor and his father a sort of specialist in Shakespearean drama on one hand, Yeats' poetry on the other, besides being the Hindi translator of Rubbaiyat of Omar Khayyam, which only exposed Amitabh to a vast ocean of literature in English as well as in Hindi. Their home in Allahabad was often visited by eminent poets like Firaq Gorakhpuri, Agneya and Sumitranandan Pant. The exposure to literature and poetry and to Shakespeare gives Amitabh Bachchan an excellent command over both, English as well as Hindi, with the perfect accent and diction.

With such a social background, when Amitabh Bachchan arrived on the scene of the Hindi film industry, he found himself indeed to be of a class which is above the ones who is abound in that industry. No one in the film industry went even an inch out of the way to accommodate Amitabh Bachchan and he had his own share of bitter struggle amidst humiliation and rejection, failures and disappointments and what is worse is that after a rise in fortunes after *Anand* in 1969, his luck ran out again in a string of flops which included *Pyar ki Kahani*, *Bansi Birju*, *Ek Nazar* and even *Parwana*. We mention *Parwana* with caution because it was this film by Joti Swarup that made Salim Javed notice Amitabh Bachchan as the face they were looking for. Similarly, his fights with the goons in S Ramanathan's *Bombay to Goa* in 1972 recommended his case highly to Prakash Mehra for *Zanjeer* that went on the floor that year. No one had much to rave about his looks as he was much too thin and much too tall, his eyes were wide and sunk deep into the sockets and skin a tad oily and dark but they all saw his confidence. I think that the confidence that Amitabh exudes comes mostly from his elated sense of social entitlements.

Jaya Bhaduri

Mrs Jaya Bachchan, now 68 years old, was born as Jaya Bhaduri in a Bengali family in Bhopal, Madhya Pradesh. In the parlance of Bengalis, the family would be known as a probashi bangali, or a non-resident Bengali. Her parents were Indira and Tarun Bhaduri, he being a man of cultural eminence. He wrote very interesting books on the now marginalised segments of the population, namely the dacoits of Chambal and one on Umrao Jaan's daughter, Piyari. Both topics have found a ready acceptance as material in Bollywood cinema. The probasi enjoys a certain freedom from the ghetto of their own culture elites and hence, they usually have freer minds and larger exposures to lands and people. They have certain smartness about them which comes from their having mixed more widely and being less restrained by a need to conform to the standards of cultures at home. They are said to have better developed personalities, a quality that comes from a greater autonomy as individuals away, from the constant need to belong to a group. Jaya Bhaduri's upbringing must be placed in this background.

Tarun Bhaduri was not only a man of letters but also well-positioned in life having occupied important posts in the government departments. Unlike Harivanshrai, Amitabh's father, who cultivated political connections especially with Nehru and Indira, Tarun Bhaduri cultivated close connections with eminent intellectuals and artists, Satyajit Ray being among them. In Bengali families such as the Bhaduris, cultivating politicians is looked down upon; however, having connections with freedom fighters is laudable. The Bhaduris were connected to Netaji Subhas Chandra Bose. The family was confident with its social position. Besides, Tarun Bhaduri was a hugely popular author, especially because of the direct reportage of the lives of the dreaded dacoits of Chambal Valley. His experiences of the community, of the lives and his personal experiences of being held hostage and then shown hospitality, became oral literature for Bengalis in Bengal.

Jaya was the eldest among three girls, all of whom were educated in English-medium schools and were brought up very liberally. To understand Jaya's life as a child, one has to understand the position of a girl child in a Bengali upper-middle class, English educated and a liberal-minded family. Enormous effort in terms of money and time are spent on educating the girl child and this is not always for her to have a job. While girls are encouraged to have careers, most girls are educated to emerge as cultured and accomplished women. The level of accomplishment in a girl child adds to the prestige of the father. In such families, even during Jaya's days, marriage was usually an option, and in fact, to have an educated and well-employed unmarried girl in the family was a way of proving to the world that the father was so powerful that he did not need to heed to the norms of the society. A free girl meant that the father is unbound and unhindered by social disciplines; a father can afford not to have the girl married off and to have the girl educated and trained in the arts. In a manner of training, Jaya was also taught the Bharat Natyam, albeit she never pursued the art seriously. She also joined the NCC.[1]

Jaya's writings in the India Memory Project vindicate the above thesis, especially in which she speaks of her father's displeasure with the usual run–of-the-mill popular films and insisted that if Jaya was really interested in cinema, she should try and work

1 https://www.youtube.com/watch?v=fco3OAkQJus

with Satyajit Ray. This is how her father took her to the famous director, and she acted in his film, *Mahanagar*. However, unlike Rekha, who at the age of 13 was forced into the film industry as the bread winner of her family, at the very same age of 13, Jaya was taken by her father to meet her famous Manik Kaku(Satyajit Ray to the world) for the purposes of pursuing her talents. Jaya also speaks of how her father chose a white Banarasi saree for his sister's wedding against the convention of red saris, and this speaks volumes of the liberal outlook and the high culture of her parental family. She was the gold medalist of her batch at Pune's famous Film and Television Institute of India, or the FTII.[2]

Barely five feet tall and petite Jaya Bhaduri came into Hindi films as one of its most promising new generation and a new-age female actor. She joined the cinema at a moment of its major transformation, a desire for a newness of feel and flavour. Bollywood was looking for newness ever since Shammi Kapoor was invented. Rauf Ahmed indicates that Geeta Bali, then the wife of Shammi Kapoor, was instrumental in inventing the image. It was her foresight that gave Hindi films Shammi Kapoor and through him, a pure image for the screen; an image unmixed from the heavy doses of ideology. Shammi was the dancing hero, a hero who was free in expressing love and unhindered in the expression of his sexuality, and despite the fact that he would dominate the screen with his almost haywire movements and a hefty body, he, paradoxically, created opportunities for beautiful women. Raj Kapoor and Dilip Kumar were intense and principled men who very decent, moralistic and idealistic females could match. But Shammi created spaces for women who simply looked good and desirable. Women came to dominate the Hindi film in the middle of the 1960s and Saira Banu, Asha Parekh, Tanuja, Vimmi, Sadhna and Waheeda Rehman and later Rakhi, Yogeeta Bali and Rekha simply rushed in. The gush of heroines was also accommodated very well in Dev Anand's films, again a hero who could just about be cast opposite any woman. Jaya Bhaduri came

2 https://www.youtube.com/watch?v=0qJ_KVtR4yw&t=214s

into this space created for women-dominated cinema, albeit towards its close.

Jaya starred in films in which she dominated; these films were even named after her. *Guddi* and *Mili* in Hindi and *Dhanni Meye* in Bengali were for her. She was Anamika in the film *Anamika*, literally meaning the nameless, in which she is an intruder who seduces the hero. In the remake of the *Sound of Music*, *Parichay*, she plays the role of the oldest girl in love with the male tutor. The film is called *Parichay*, or an introduction, which is her introduction to a romantic arousing. *Piya Ka Ghar* was about her adjustments into her in-laws house. *Abhiman* was her *abhiman* in Hrishikesh Mukherjee's film by the same name.[3]

The heroine-centred roles were about emotions, especially about adolescence that is slowly transformed into adulthood. She was young and short, petite and delicate, like a pre-pubertal girl, and her roles were the soft and sweet romances of the sixteen, in which her growing up constituted the rhythm and tune of the narrative. Expectedly, therefore, Jaya's films would often deliver some of the greatest hits of Bollywood music. R.D.Burman, it may well be said, rose from films in which Jaya starred; his music essentially carried the soul of the adolescent slowly blooming to her adulthood.

Jaya had no worries about earning for her family, and indeed, as among Indians in general and Bengalis in particular a working woman is often pitied as being an underprivileged hag who had the misfortune not to be provided by a male of her family. Interestingly, in the film *Mahanagar*, Jaya's maiden venture with Satyajit Ray, the theme centred on a housewife who was forced to enter the job market when her husband's factory was closed down. Jaya was the sister of the unfortunate man in the story. It is likely that for women in her position earning an income was essentially a matter of misfortune, though in another modernist thought system, the economic independence for women and

3 *Abhiman* in Hindi means pride but in Bengali it means to be hurt. Hrishikesh Mukherjee used the term to depict Jaya's sense of hurt at her husband's egoistic behavior.

that too through a career that gives fame was also looming as a prospect. Jaya remained torn between these two diametrically opposite poles; whether to revel in luxury in the comforts of home raising children and looking after the kitchen or whether to emerge on her own upon the world with roles that would make people remember her for the times to come. This dilemma, a national dilemma of India, chases women even to this day, and may remain India's defining dilemma for centuries to come.

As long as Amitabh was a struggling actor and Jaya and he were intensely in love with each other, things were perfect for her. Jaya, in her utter love for Amitabh Bachchan, carried him around quite a bit. They starred together disastrously in B.R.Ishara's film, *Ek Nazar* and also in Prakash Verma's *Bansi Birju*, both of which saw Jaya in the role of a prostitute, totally unsuitable for her image. Both productions were small and B grade and despite Jaya Bhaduri being a big star of the times, she compromised on the choice of films only to work with Amitabh Bachchan. When gossip mills went agog with Amitabh and Jaya's romance, Amitabh told Stardust 'Stop Telling Those Lies about Us', not wanting to acknowledge the romance.[4]

This was unfortunate because Jaya was sacrificing her time by doing movies that would accommodate Amitabh Bachchan. Jaya's power in the industry can well be understood by her tiff with the director, B.R. Ishara over a rape scene in the film. The scene required Jaya's clothes to be torn off, to which she objected. Ishara threatened to report her behavior to the artists' council, ensuring that she be given no work in the industry, to which Jaya did not relent. Eventually, Ishara made peace with his leading lady. Hence, it was only to accommodate Amitabh in her life that Jaya approached those who would cast her boyfriend along with her. She was the one who led the relationship.[5]

Amitabh Bachchan, as an aspiring actor, too chose the highbrow cinema as his calling, for he went to Mrinal Sen in

4 Cover Story. Stardust. Mumbai. March 1973.

5 https://www.youtube.com/watch?v=Toj3fnTVbMU

Kolkata for an opportunity. Amitabh had taken lessons in Bengali as a part of his career in his office and tried to negotiate with Mrinal Sen that he actually knew the language. Mrinal Sen used Amitabh's excellent voice to have him as a voiceover narrator for *Bhuvan Shome*. The credits simply acknowledged an 'Amitabh' in the title cards. Later, Amitabh rose into prominence with Hrishikesh Mukherjee's *Anand*, also a middle of the road film, in which he supported the main star, the reigning superstar, Rajesh Khanna. Things dipped for Amitabh Bachchan after his success in *Anand* and in his darkest days, Jaya stood by him, trying to prop up his career. But those days Amitabh was with Jaya, in her kind of circle, among her kind of cinema. It was not until he met up with Salim-Javed that Amitabh really discovered his cosmic goal, to develop into the image of the angry young man who was to shake the universe of the Hindi film from its very core like a massive earthquake.

It was in his rise to stardom that Jaya and Amitabh fell apart; for Jaya, Amitabh's success ended her need in his career. It was not merely success, but in success, Amitabh emerged a different man, an angry man, a street fighter, violent, fallen off his class, living among the crass, exiled, tragic, lonely and deeply immersed in the sorrows of the world. In this image, he also rose as the superstar; from being Jaya's husband and the father of their children, he suddenly belonged to everybody and strangely, to nobody.

Note: For an excellent biography of Jaya Bachchan, please see, Soumya Bandopadhyay's Amitabh Bachchan by Ananda Publishers, 1995.

Jaya's Videos

I have a YouTube clip from 1983, an interview of Amitabh Bachchan along with Jaya aired for the BBC. Amitabh is aloof, confident, speaking in a tone of supreme authority about his films, his accident on the sets of *Coolie*, his family background and why he does the kind of films he does. Jaya sits beside him, totally demure, surrendered to his aura, quiet, obedient, without even looking at him, supporting all that he says and sometimes a little surprised at not knowing some minor facts about his career. (https://www.youtube.com/watch?v=kiotjvY81y4&t=793s&index=2&list=PL2iHSrsp8QJvkUhlvIPUEkUgw9RNSoR8C)

Then I see yet another video clip from 1990 shot in the UK shot by the BBC in which Amitabh is again supremely confident, patronisingly looking at those around him. Ladies rush to be clicked by his side, Jaya is just another one of them. Amitabh looks literally 'down upon them' due to his great height, smiles at them and then completely focuses on his own face being shot by the camera.(https://www.youtube.com/watch?v=TJfi4jcUfl8&t=347s&index=4&list=PL2iHSrsp8QJvkUhlvIPUEkUgw9RNSoR8C)

I see Nasreen Munni Kabir's *Follow That Star* documentary in which Jaya comes in for the first time on screen for an interview. She is on her own now, all by herself, facing the camera. She speaks about Amitabh Bachchan, seemingly overawed by her husband, but betraying also a need to emerge on her own. I think that the camera turns on the artist in her; she desires to break forth. This video is after Amitabh resigns from politics, and Jaya, despite her exposure to people and politicians, is still guarded, and as if bound by some oath to be diplomatically measured in her speech. Yet, she reveals herself to be one of extreme likes and dislikes. (https://www.youtube.com/watch?v=kUoXqoWkA9c&t=111s)

I see her in Simi Garewal's Rendevous in 1998 where Simi starts the interview with Jaya who is still very inhibited and she mumbles and is at loss of words; Amitabh Bachchan is articulate, constantly speaking in to fill her long gaps and silences. In 2012, she is far more open and vocal and here she is with her children; she looks more protected against her very articulate husband. Jaya calls Amitabh an UPite as well and gives away his rural habits of oiling their children's hair. (https://www.youtube.com/watch?v=jtq67J95QtU&list=PL2iHSrsp8QJvkUhlvIPUEkUgw9RNSoR8C&index=47&t=255s and https://www.youtube.com/watch?v=KTjrTSd2TkI&list=PL2iHSrsp8QJvkUhlvIPUEkUgw9-RNSoR8C&index=48&t=294s)

In the interview in 2012 for NDTV Good Times by Abu Jani and Sandeep, Jaya is refreshingly fresh, forthcoming, humorous, intelligent and even entertaining. She speaks of a self that is Jaya Bhaduri and not Jaya Bachchan. The latter is a demure person, restrained and inhibited, while the person she repressed wanted to be in foreign affairs, in the world of the civil services. Films just happened to her and just that. She drifted into cinema and from there to marriage with Amitabh Bachchan, which was a love at first sight. (https://www.youtube.com/watch?v=oqJ_KVtR4yw&list=PL2iHSrsp8QJvkUhlvIPUEkUgw9RNSoR8C&index=49&t=188s)

In 2013, in the Walk the Talk with Shekhar Gupta on the campus of the FTII, we see an enormously confident Jaya, reminiscing about her days at the Institute, remembering moments of joy; her memory seemed to be alert and she is assertive of her likes and dislikes. (https://www.youtube.com/watch?v=2eXFbmAM07U&t=20s)

By the time we are in 2016, Jaya's voice becomes downright scurrilous. She is irritable, dismissive, arrogant, and rude and thinks of nothing of what she speaks. She seems to lose her decency. She is ill-tempered at award functions; she is rude in the Kapil Sharma show. It seems as if she is breaking free of her marriage, her shackles of propriety. These videos show that she is now no-holds-barred and has had enough and now seeks freedom. She is done with her duties as a wife, a mother, a daughter-in-law; she has no career to look forward to, no household chores to look after. Her bad temper is just her impatience with the confines of her image, her social role, her status, and her anger at the press exhibits her desire to break totally free of whatever had contained her for so long. (https://www.youtube.com/watch?v=jFKBa5bBdeM&t=41s&list=PL2iHSrsp8QJvkUhlvIPUEkUgw9-RNSoR8C&index=21)

Homemaker

I have been an Amitabh fan and then a follower and then an observer since 1975. It was my intense desire to crack the code of his popularity. My opportunity came in 1989 when I wrote an MPhil dissertation on the superstar in the JNU. I sent a copy of my work to Amitabh and it impressed him enormously that I got an invitation to be his house guest. At his house, Amitabh wanted to know me better, my mind and where I got this unbelievable sense of what he was like. I was amused at his surprise because, to me, he was not an unknown entity; minds always work in patterns and because I was a fan, I knew that his mind worked like my own. I told him so only to confuse him further.

Amitabh's home was just the way I conjured up in my mind. It was organised more like an office, arranged to deliver work spaces, thought spaces, reading spaces so that one could sit anywhere and work. Prateeksha was not very large in terms of persons per square foot, yet it was planned in great detail to create large visual areas and light. The food was immaculate, the menu elaborate and the entire family descended upon me to supervise my wellbeing. I felt as if I was a guru visiting the devotee home. There could be nothing more perfect for a fan than this. I told Amitabh that I was the only person apart from Yudhisthira from Mahabharata to have walked into Heaven in flesh and blood.

But what I saw of Amitabh Bachchan that blew me away was him as a homemaker. He was involved in everything; from the planning of the menu, to notice what my eating preferences were, to whether I had enough of pickle to whet my palette, whether I needed to go to the bathroom, whether I was feeling cold or hot, whether the sun was hitting my face, whether I got enough of every dish prepared, whether I was being polite enough to respect the sweets his mother sent for us as prasad; for once I thought that looking after me was Amitabh's prime job. And amidst all of this, he was taking stock of car servicing, calling up people like Javed Akhtar to give me interviews, inaugurating a woman's boutique, appearing for television interviews, planning for Shammi Kapoor's television journal, arranging a trip to South Africa where he was to perform and rehearse. I have always found it difficult to balance home life and work life, found it difficult to look after my dear ones and manage my various submissions at the same time and space. I indeed marvel at the ability of Amitabh to keep track of hundreds of details in each passing moment of everyday life. I think he has a highly-endowed mental capacity which is clearly beyond me. Academically and intellectually I may be miles ahead of him though.

Jaya felt that I needed to plan my time better; she suggested that I gave money to the cook, after all how much could he steal, so that he could get my vegetables and I would could get more time for work.

She immediately noticed that I was fond of tea, made endless cups for me while chatting about how Amitabh was totally wrong in leaving politics, and thus, in a way, letting down his electorate. In my eyes, I did not see Jaya bother so much with homemaking as Amitabh was. Amitabh's eyes seemed to be everywhere, taking stock of medicines for his parents, checking on with the injections for his father, scolding his servants for not closing the window panes in the evening because a mosquito had bit me. Jaya was the more relaxed person and I wished I had some time to exclusively chat with her. I thought that she could be an interesting person to know but she was too absorbed in her role as a royalty to emerge as an independent entity. She had a look in her eyes, a look I have seen in many women who need to fall into the boundaries of their in-laws and to conform to the role they fill in. I felt like smuggling out my phone number to her so that she could call me up; I think that I should have.

My Journey With Amitabh Bachchan, As Amitabh Bachchan

I first "saw" Amitabh Bachchan when I was on a vacation in Chennai, then called Madras to visit my extended family. He was there in the form of a pin up poster in the bathroom door of my cousin who seemed to be totally enamoured by the man with sunken cheeks and deep set eyes. My cousin said that she liked him because he, like her was too tall to be good looking. He, she said, was a film star. That was a time when *Anand* had just been released and it seems that he played the role of a melancholic doctor in the film. The age belonged to Rajesh Khanna and it was he who we all knew as the heartthrob of the country. Amitabh Bachchan, was just a man too thin with a Bengali sounding name. Slowly, data started flowing in the air about the new guy as he been a man with a respectable background and one who left a plush job in Kolkata, then Calcutta to act in films, a rather strange mobility of occupations, I thought. My family in Kolkata hardly ever looked beyond Rabindranath Tagore and barely had much to do with the cinema. We only read books for entertainment or listened to the radio. Whatever little of films I watched, I really liked Jaya Bhaduri and when I heard that Amitabh was her boyfriend I noticed him a little more on the covers of the film magazines when I passed the pavements of my locality.

I "met" Amitabh forty years ago while watching *Sholay* after it already had run over two years. After that I quickly watched *Amar Akbar Anthony*. I watched *Zanjeer* and *Deewar* much later in reruns. Thereafter, I tracked Amitabh through both the new releases as well as the rereleases of older movies. I decided that I was Amitabh Bachchan, in my mind every separation between his entity and mine was to vanish. I had to think with his thoughts, move with his body language and work through my everyday life as if, within my own precincts I was he. I was not romantically nor erotically attracted to him; my attraction towards him was philosophical.

Sholay, cannot really be said to belong to Amitabh specifically yet there was something about him for which I decided that in my life henceforth, I will be Amitabh Bachchan. I grew studious, dead serious, somewhat melancholic, but focused and decided to win at everything I do. I became a perfectionist, hardworking, confident, defiant and also arrogant. I used to imagine Amitabh Bachchan as bearing all of the above attributes and hence worked myself up to be all of these. Slowly, I discovered that the image of the star also was attached to his parents, dutiful towards his children and I too, taught myself to be mindful of my own parents. When I watched *Deewar*, I became intensely political; interestingly, I developed a socialist, egalitarian, anti-rich political affiliation with strong ideas about social justice. I trained myself to become fearless and soon had a hostile body language that helped me hold out against potential eve teasers.

Then came Amitabh's first downfall as he, charged with graft, resigned from politics. I became aware of the sociology of public opinion and since I was about to write my MPhil examinations in JNU, I decided to work on the public condemnation of Amitabh Bachchan. My thesis was called the *Social Construction of a Hero, The Images By Amitabh Bachchan*. In the dissertation I discussed how the star image of Amitabh Bachchan made the public construct him as a man who could corrupt the politicians.

I started working at the end of the career as an MPhil student and soon I used Amitabh's formula of hitting back at critics with a slew of comeback films, renewed contacts with the media and creating noise around his own victimization as the apt formula which I could use against harassment at my workplace. I started feeling invincible in the sense that if I do not accept defeat, no one can rile me in. I learnt how to rise up against hostilities. My MPhil dissertation expanded into a PhD thesis in which I concentrated on how Amitabh Bachchan was a philosophy of overcoming of obstacles and of evolving into a higher level of achievements.

It was exactly on the 20th of December 1990 that I got an invitation from Amitabh Bachchan to be his house guest at Prateeksha in Mumbai. The invitation came through a call from Mumbai, then still Bombay in my landlord's telephone because I as yet did not have my own connection. It seems that he called earlier in the day while I was at office, wanted to know when I would be available "directly" to take his call and there I was at 10 minutes past 6 pm to talk to him. I told him that trains were full in the last week of December and that I might like to postpone my visit until later into the New Year but he said that he was to visit South Africa and then again get very busy so here he was in a lean period when breaks were manageable. He would send me plane tickets both ways, the return being an open ticket and I was not to worry because I would be very well taken care of at his house by his family and him. But the nights, I said I would want to be in my office guest house, fairly close to his house in Juhu because I was not too comfortable living in with families which included even my own relatives. I was duly booked for the nights at the airport Hotel, fully paid for by Amitabh Bachchan. The reason for the invitation was that I had posted him, albeit rather late, copies of my MPhil dissertation from JNU titled the *Social Construction of a Hero –Images By Amitabh Bachchan*. The stuff I wrote, he said were exactly presented just in the way he thought of himself in his mind. How could I ever know his mind so well was the curiosity he wished to satiate through my visit to his home.

Though such an invitation from Amitabh Bachchan to be a guest at his very home would be nothing short of Yudhisthir's privilege of walking straight into Heaven in flesh and blood, yet by then I had become so familiar with his persona and so much thinking like him that I feared that such complete an agreement would leave me with nothing to dialogue on. Frankly, I no longer needed to meet Amitabh. But I would get a chance to see Jaya Bhaduri, and to see her became my overriding interest in visiting Prateeksha.

Amitabh sent over the tickets to me through his establishment in Delhi and his car and driver picked me up in the wee hours of the morning to drop me at the airport for the flight to Mumbai. I was more worried about a packet of soft *notun gur* sweets not being squashed on flight that I was carrying for the Bachchan family purchased from Annapurna in front of their Delhi bungalow, Sopan. Then finally as the day broke and life picked up in the streets in Mumbai that his car drove me into Prateeksha. Amitabh was the first person to greet me in the house. He was getting very distracted by a light sweater that I was wearing from Delhi because though Delhi was freezing, Mumbai was hot. He constantly worried that should the sun become brighter I would sweat. He then took the journalist who was interviewing him and me into the wooden shed at the corner of his garden because here he could run the air-conditioning. He was more enthusiastic talking about my work to the journalist than about discussing his.

It was close to lunch that I met the family in full force which included Ajitabh who had come down from London. I soon realized as we sat down to dine in the finest silver crockery and over a twelve course meal, that it was not Amitabh Bachchan, but I who was the star. Eyes were looking at me admiringly and with awe, there were furtive glances from the staff trying to see what kind of a star I was so as to merit such an honour. I inferred that so far no guest has been so much honoured at Prateeksha as I was. Perhaps the reason was that I was an academic and so was Harivanshrai Bachchan. Teji, Amitabh's mother told me that

Harivanshrai had read my work and then my bibliography and said to her that so many books, even he had not read. I was being admired for my academic achievement.

In my observations and through my analyses of Amitabh Bachchan, he, his family, his home, the way it was organized, the décor, and his daily routine was very familiar to me. It was as if I knew them as closely as I knew my own family. But it was interesting that they too found me familiar to them as well. I think that they knew my "type", intelligentsia, city bred urban middle class educated in premier institutions with excellent schooling and that made my "type" much more familiar to the family than the film world of Mumbai could ever be.

Yes, food was resplendent and overflowing, Amitabh was perceptive to my addiction to pickles and insisted that the pickle should always be set before me for all meals. Jaya was torn between being a good host and just chatting with me finding in me a fellow Bengali who remembered her glorious films and her famous Bengali directors. But the memory that I would cherish were the philosophical discussions with Amitabh and Jaya over the nature of self, manifestations of ego, anger, morality, the law and justice, democracy and ethics, stardom and cinema, poetry and epic, spectacle and extravaganza, violence and obscenity, right wing politics and liberalism, vendetta of the media and the emancipatory power of popular culture, of Hussain and Ganesh Pyne, of eyes and laughter, of image and appeal. My research on the cinema and stardom have mainly revolved around reflections of these discussions, most of these I have captured in this book of sixty essays around the image of Amitabh Bachchan.

Eventually my MPhil grew into my PhD part of which emerged to the world as my book published by Penguin called Amitabh – The Making of a Superstar modelled on Hegel's Phenomenology of the Spirit and Logic, I would use Amitabh's formula of hitting back at critics. Just as Amitabh retaliated with a slew of comeback films, renewed contacts with the media and creating noise around his own victimization as the apt formula, I shot into a flurry of writings, research and visibility in conferences to stand up to harassment in workplace. I started feeling invincible in the sense that if I do not accept defeat, no one can rile me in. I learnt how to rise up against hostilities into victory, just as Amitabh would do in cinema and in his life.

Slowly I grew older and more settled in my employment and made a name for myself in my career. I now own my own apartment and drive my own car; my days as a street fighter seems to be over. I also have now other people to admire, I no longer watch popular films, and I have expanded my readings far beyond political thoughts into reading more of history and anthropology. I no longer need to be Amitabh Bachchan and Amitabh, truly seems to have brought me as far as he could and now my journey with him seems to be over. When I look back on the star with distance and detachment and again ask myself the same question, what makes Amitabh into the star that he is, I find that it is neither action nor anger, neither victory nor vengeance, neither renewal nor retribution, neither comedy nor tragedy, neither the victor, nor the victim that made his image. If there is one word with which to really describe him then it is restrain. He seems to live at the limit and yet is strangely self-contained, being neither ecstatic in joy nor desperate in sorrow, money does not embolden him, and penury does not unsettle him. When in bad times, he thinks of emerging out and when in good times, he dreams of further perfection. Such self-command cannot come without a very great level of self-awareness and now if I am to become Amitabh again, then I will have to raise my consciousness and not my anger.